Weight-Free Exercises

Weight-Free Exercises

Hollis Liebman

hinkler

Published by Hinkler Books Pty Ltd 2017
45–55 Fairchild Street
Heatherton Victoria 3202 Australia
www.hinkler.com

hinkler

Copyright © Hinkler Books Pty Ltd 2017

Created by Moseley Road Inc.
President: Sean Moore
General Manager: Karen Prince
Editor: Jo Weeks
Designer: Tina Vaughan

Photographer: FineArtsPhotoGroup.com
Models: Joseph Benedict, Jillian Langenau
Illustrator: Hector Aiza/3DLabz
Prepress: Splitting Image

ISBN: 978 1 4889 3440 7

Printed and bound in China

Always do the warm-up exercises before attempting any individual exercises. It is recommended that you check with
your doctor or healthcare professional before commencing any exercise regime. While every care has been taken in
the preparation of this material, the publishers and their respective employees or agents will not accept responsibility
for injury or damage occasioned to any person as a result of participation in the activities described in this book.

Contents

Working Out

Although weight rooms and gyms are commonplace, some people prefer to keep fit and improve their muscle tone in the privacy of their home, or in a quiet moment at work.

If you are one of these people, be assured that it is not unusual. Whether it is because you are put off by the social aspect of a busy gym, having to be around people you don't know, facing the inevitable queues and fights over limited equipment, or the cost of the membership fee itself—whatever the reason, if you don't want to go to the gym, you don't have to go.

But without a gym, can you develop a body that is not only nice to look at, but is also fitter and more able to do what you would like it to do?

The answer, of course, is yes. The problem lies in avoiding the gym but doing nothing else instead. Much like a car, the human body is built to be used. It isn't meant to lie around doing nothing. Without regular use and maintenance, a car becomes gradually less reliable and eventually ceases to function. The same goes for our bodies. If we don't work at keeping them strong and limber, we will begin to lose muscle strength and body flexibility, particularly later on in life, and this could lead to difficulty in simply getting around.

How to do a weight-free workout

This book is intended for those people who want to be fit, but don't want to go to the gym. In addition to a wide variety of resistance-training exercises, the book contains routines that focus on stretching, mobility, balance, and cardio workouts. The exercises have been formulated to be done without the aid of any special equipment. Put simply, you use the weight of your body to build your strength and endurance. An exercise mat, a chair, and some loose clothing, along with a good pair of trainers, are all you need.

It's obvious when you think about it: Because your body is always with you, if you learn to use it as an instrument for exercise, you can carry out a fitness routine almost anywhere. Whether it is at home, at work, in a park, all you need is yourself and your imagination (or this book), and you can have a complete and satisfying workout. And because you are using your body weight to work out, you can change the loads and stress placed on it at will.

Being self-sufficient as an exercise machine means you don't need to wait around for a gym partner, who may never turn up, you don't have to queue for a spot on the bench, nor do you even have to go to the gym at all.

Combine muscle-toning exercises with body stretches, such as the classic Cobra.

With today's busy schedule and hectic demands, maneuvering life to find time for the gym can be pretty tough, so being able to fit in a few exercises whenever and wherever could be a real game-changer for you in your search for a fully fit and functional body.

Start by reading through all the exercises in the book. Some will be familiar to you, others less so, and there will be some that you have never tried before. They are rated by their relative difficulty. However, this is just a guide—you may find some easier or more difficult than others, simply because of your own current levels of fitness. If you do a sport that works your upper body, for example, you should find those exercises that focus on upper-body

strength and fitness easier to do. By really exploring this book and implementing, on a regular basis, its methodologies and strategies, you will maximize your potential. Remember, both the plan (this book) and the equipment (your body) are about as portable as they can get.

To sum up, *Weight-Free Excercises* is for everyone who wants to be fit and healthy. It's a detailed catalogue of exercises for people of any age or fitness level who want to feel good walking up stairs, running for the bus, or reaching for the top shelf and cultivate a beautiful body along the way.

Choose exercises that you can do at your desk or in the kitchen, such as Chair Abdominal Crunch.

Work out wherever and whenever you want and you will soon see a change in your body.

Full-Body Anatomy

Annotation Key
* indicates deep muscles

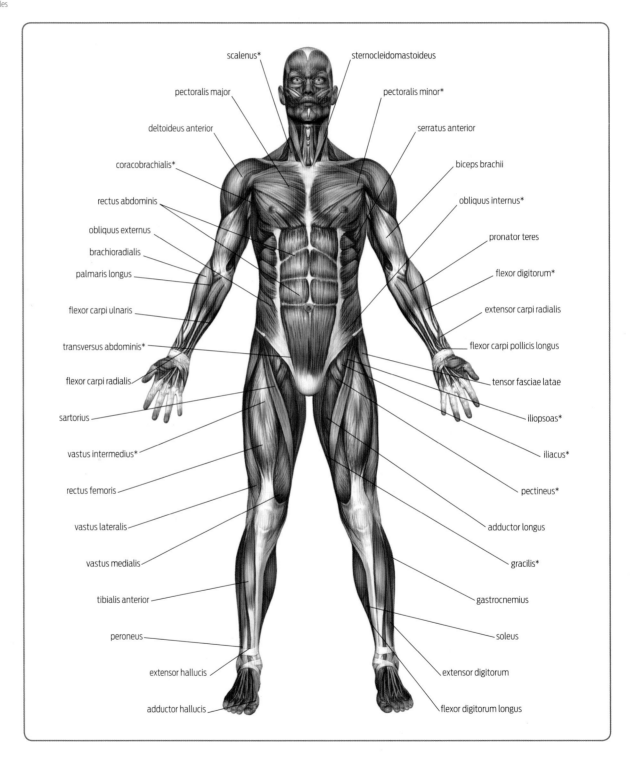

scalenus*

sternocleidomastoideus

pectoralis major

pectoralis minor*

deltoideus anterior

serratus anterior

coracobrachialis*

biceps brachii

rectus abdominis

obliquus internus*

obliquus externus

pronator teres

brachioradialis

flexor digitorum*

palmaris longus

extensor carpi radialis

flexor carpi ulnaris

flexor carpi pollicis longus

transversus abdominis*

tensor fasciae latae

flexor carpi radialis

iliopsoas*

sartorius

iliacus*

vastus intermedius*

pectineus*

rectus femoris

adductor longus

vastus lateralis

gracilis*

vastus medialis

gastrocnemius

tibialis anterior

soleus

peroneus

extensor hallucis

extensor digitorum

adductor hallucis

flexor digitorum longus

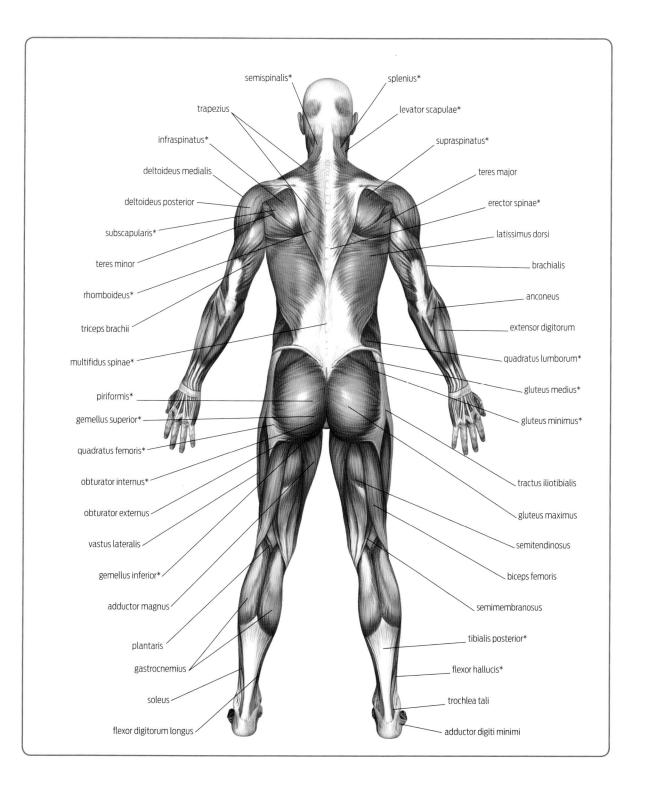

semispinalis*

splenius*

trapezius

levator scapulae*

infraspinatus*

supraspinatus*

deltoideus medialis

teres major

deltoideus posterior

erector spinae*

subscapularis*

latissimus dorsi

teres minor

brachialis

rhomboideus*

anconeus

triceps brachii

extensor digitorum

multifidus spinae*

quadratus lumborum*

piriformis*

gluteus medius*

gemellus superior*

gluteus minimus*

quadratus femoris*

obturator internus*

tractus iliotibialis

obturator externus

gluteus maximus

vastus lateralis

semitendinosus

gemellus inferior*

biceps femoris

adductor magnus

semimembranosus

plantaris

tibialis posterior*

gastrocnemius

flexor hallucis*

soleus

trochlea tali

flexor digitorum longus

adductor digiti minimi

Contents

Stretching is vital to physical performance and state of being. It has myriad benefits, including increased range of motion, improved blood circulation, and enhanced energy levels; in short, stretching makes a major contribution to an improved quality of life. There are several stretching "groups," each serving a different purpose. Static Stretching is the most common form where a muscle is held in its maximal extended state for 30 seconds or more. Dynamic Stretching involves a movement done continuously through a range of motion, often mimicking athletic performance for sport. Ballistic Stretching is done explosively and through repeated bouncy movement for athletic endeavors. There is much debate on when it is best to stretch—before or after exercise? In my opinion, it should be done after and during a routine, when the muscles are warm and pliable. Stretching when muscles are cold may result in injury. It is best to do at least a light warm-up, such as stationary cycling, prior to stretching.

Stretches

Iliotibial Band Stretch

Stretching the iliotibial (IT) band is rather different from stretching other muscles, as the IT band is a thick, fibrous fascia without the elasticity of your muscles. Iliotibial band stretches can make a great difference to back, hip, and knee problems.

Correct form
· Be sure to ease into the movement slowly.

Avoid
· Overextending your legs.
· Locking your knees.

1 Start in a standing position, and cross your left foot behind the right ankle.

2 Lean forward until your fingertips are as close to the floor as you can get them. If you are able, grasp your toes, or—more difficult—place your hands flat on the floor.

3 Hold for 20 seconds and repeat, then switch legs and repeat the entire stretch.

Back View

- tractus iliotibialis
- gluteus maximus
- vastus lateralis
- semitendinosus
- biceps femoris
- semimembranosus

Front View

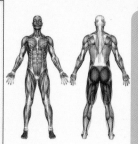

Level
· Beginner

Duration
· 1½–2 minutes

Benefits
· Increases range of hip movement
· Counteracts effects of wearing high heels

Caution
· Neck issues
· Hip or knee issues
· Lower-back pain

- gluteus maximus
- tractus iliotibialis
- biceps femoris
- gastrocnemius

Modification

Easier: If you cannot touch the floor, reach down as far as is comfortable and grasp your legs. With practice you will find you can reach lower.

Piriformis Stretch

This move targets the gluteal and hip regions, and takes around two minutes to complete. The piriformis muscle laterally rotates and stabilizes the hip, and is particularly used in sports that require sudden changes of direction.

Correct form
· Be sure to ease into the movement slowly.
· Relax your hips to enable a deeper stretch.

Avoid
· Pulling your thigh to your chest forcefully or jerkily.

1 Lie on your back with your legs bent.

2 Cross your right ankle over your left knee.

3 Use your hands to grab the back of the left thigh close to the knee, and gently pull it toward your right shoulder. Hold for 30 seconds, relax, and then hold for another 30 seconds, then switch sides.

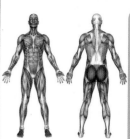

Level
· Beginner

Duration
· 2 minutes

Benefits
· Mobilizes the hips, piriformis, glutes, and lower back

Caution
· Shoulder issues
· Hip issues
· Lower-back pain

Annotation Key
* indicates deep muscles

piriformis*

gluteus minimus*

gluteus maximus

quadratus femoris*

Cobra Stretch

This stretch helps loosen the spinal joints, and stretches your stomach, upper torso muscles, and the spine. It is a good overall stretch, but avoid it if you have had back issues of any sort.

Correct form
· Keep your arms close to your sides.

Avoid
· An excessive upward swing.
· Tensing your buttocks.
· Splaying your elbows out to the sides.

1 Lie facedown with your arms bent, your elbows in, and your palms on the ground.

2 Lift your upper body until your arms are at full length, bending your torso backward.

3 Complete 3 repetitions of 15 seconds each.

Back View

erector
spinae*

quadratus
lumborum

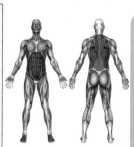

Level
· Intermediate

Duration
· 1–2 minutes

Benefits
· Helps loosen the
  spinal joints
· Stretches chest, abs,
  and shoulders

Caution
· Lower-back pain
· Wrist issues

Annotation Key
* indicates deep muscles

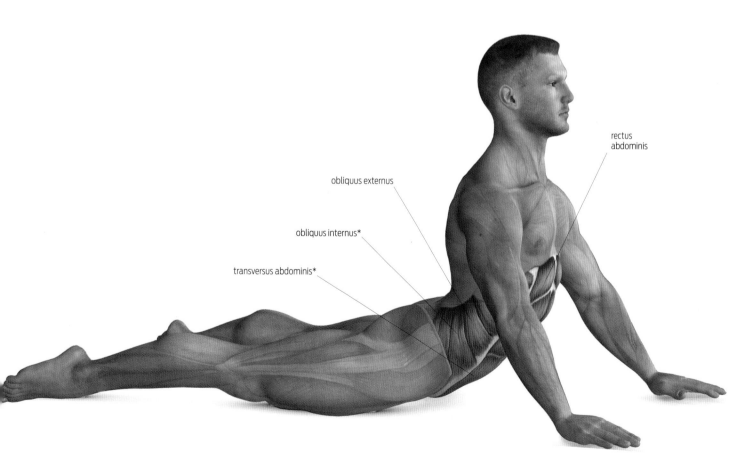

rectus
abdominis

obliquus externus

obliquus internus*

transversus abdominis*

Hip-to-Thigh Stretch

Your hip flexors enable you to lift your knees and to bend at the waist. They are located on your upper thighs, just below your hip bones. This exercise particularly targets both the hip flexors and the adductor muscles.

1 Kneeling on your left knee, place your right foot in front of you. Have your right foot flat on the floor, your left heel lifted.

2 Shift your weight and gradually bring your torso forward, bending your right knee more deeply so that the knee shifts toward your toes. Hold your arms straight out in front.

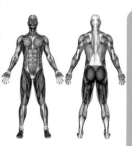

Correct form

· Your shoulders and neck should be relaxed.
· Keep your upper body stable.
· Reach up but do not force the reach.

Avoid

· Extending your front knee too far over the planted foot.
· Overstretching the thigh.

3 Keeping your torso stable, press your left hip forward until you feel a stretch over the front of your thigh.

4 Raise your arms toward the ceiling. Hold for 10 seconds, release, and repeat up to 4 more times. Switch sides and repeat.

Level
· Beginner

Duration
· 2–3 minutes

Benefits
· Stretches hips and thighs
· Improves motion in arms and legs

Caution
· Hip or groin problems
· Knee issues

Annotation Key
* indicates deep muscles

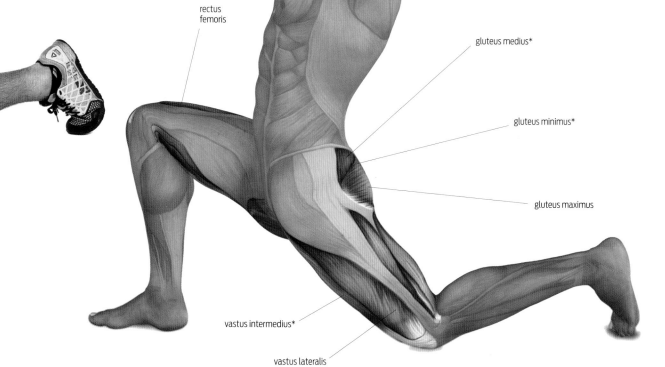

rectus femoris

gluteus medius*

gluteus minimus*

gluteus maximus

vastus intermedius*

vastus lateralis

Cat and Dog Stretch

This stretch consists of moving the spine from a rounded position (flexion) to an arched one (extension). It's a basic motion, but one that is enormously beneficial in preventing back pain and maintaining a healthy spine.

Correct form
· Draw your shoulders away from your neck.

Avoid
· Arching primarily in your lower back.

1 Begin on your hands and knees, with your wrists directly below your shoulders and your knees directly below your hips. Your fingertips should be facing forward, with your hands shoulder-width apart. Look down at the floor, keeping your head in a neutral position.

2 Exhale, and round your spine up toward the ceiling, dropping your head. Draw your belly button in toward your spine. Keep your hips lifted and your shoulders in the same position. This is the cat pose.

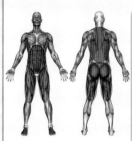

3 Inhale, and uncurl your spine.
Remain on your hands and knees.

4 With your next inhalation, arch your spine, lifting your chest forward and your tailbone toward the ceiling. Look forward. This is the dog pose.

5 Exhale, and return to a neutral position on your hands and knees.

6 Repeat the entire sequence 10–20 times.

Level
· Beginner

Duration
· 1½–2 minutes

Benefits
· Stretches shoulders, chest, abdominals, neck, and spine

Caution
· Hip issues
· Knee pain

Annotation Key
* indicates deep muscles

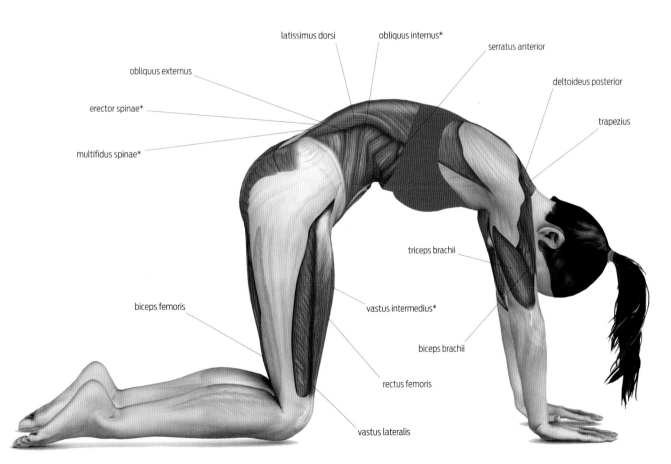

latissimus dorsi

obliquus internus*

serratus anterior

obliquus externus

deltoideus posterior

erector spinae*

trapezius

multifidus spinae*

triceps brachii

biceps femoris

vastus intermedius*

biceps brachii

rectus femoris

vastus lateralis

Toe Touch

Toe-touching is a basic exercise that provides a number of benefits. Normally performed while standing up, it works multiple muscle groups as well as offering flexibility and stretching benefits. Toe touches are also an effective cool-down exercise.

1 Stand up tall and exhale.

2 Tuck your head down toward your chest and roll down one vertebra at a time, reaching down toward your toes. Keep your weight slightly shifted forward. Continue exhaling.

Correct form
· Stack your spine one vertebra at a time.

Avoid
· Tensing your neck muscles.
· Bouncing to reach farther down.

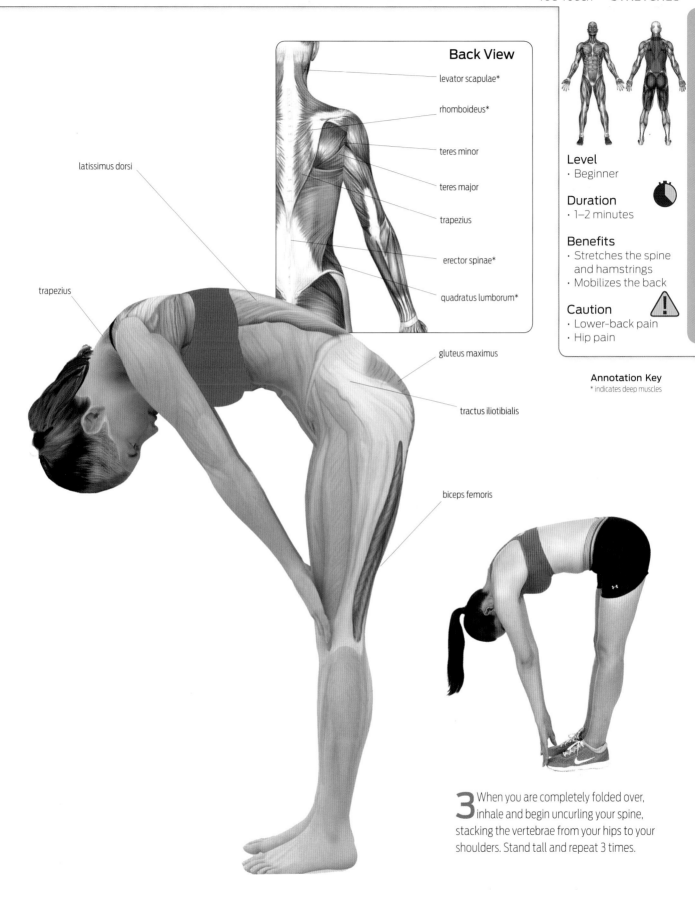

Back View

levator scapulae*

rhomboideus*

teres minor

teres major

trapezius

erector spinae*

quadratus lumborum*

latissimus dorsi

trapezius

gluteus maximus

tractus iliotibialis

biceps femoris

Level
· Beginner

Duration
· 1–2 minutes

Benefits
· Stretches the spine and hamstrings
· Mobilizes the back

Caution
· Lower-back pain
· Hip pain

Annotation Key
* indicates deep muscles

3 When you are completely folded over, inhale and begin uncurling your spine, stacking the vertebrae from your hips to your shoulders. Stand tall and repeat 3 times.

Hip Stretch

Positioning of the hip affects pelvic and spinal posture and function so the regular performance of hip stretches will help you maintain a good posture and alignment.

Correct form
· Keep your neck and shoulders relaxed.
· Apply even pressure to your leg with your active hand.

Avoid
· Rounding your torso.
· Lifting the foot of your bent leg off the floor.

1 In a seated position, extend your left leg straight in front of you, and bend your right knee.

2 Cross your bent knee over the straight leg, and keep your foot flat on the ground. Wrap your left arm around the bent knee.

3 Apply pressure to your bent knee to rotate your torso. Keep your hips aligned as you pull your chest in toward your knee.

4 Hold for 30 seconds. Slowly release, and repeat 3 times on each side.

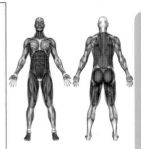

Front View

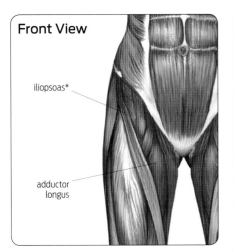

iliopsoas*

adductor longus

Back View

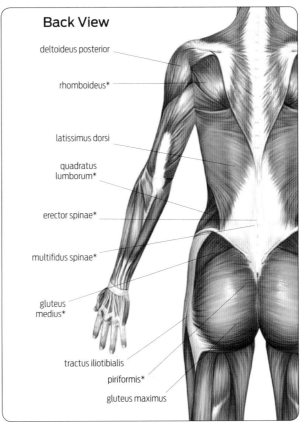

deltoideus posterior

rhomboideus*

latissimus dorsi

quadratus lumborum*

erector spinae*

multifidus spinae*

gluteus medius*

tractus iliotibialis

piriformis*

gluteus maximus

Level
· Intermediate

Duration
· 3 minutes

Benefits
· Stretches hip extensors and flexors
· Mobilizes spine

Caution
· Lower-back issues
· Shoulder pain
· Hip problems

Annotation Key
* indicates deep muscles

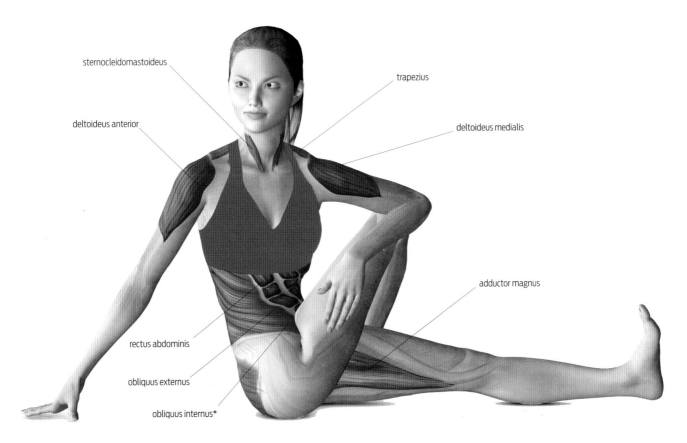

sternocleidomastoideus

deltoideus anterior

trapezius

deltoideus medialis

adductor magnus

rectus abdominis

obliquus externus

obliquus internus*

Latissimus Dorsi Stretch

The latissimus dorsi is a broad muscle that covers much of the lower back. The lats draw your arms down and back. Reaching your arms overhead stretches them. You can stretch your lats while sitting, standing, or kneeling. Using a wall or table can help intensify the stretch.

Correct form
· Elongate your arms and shoulders as much as possible.

Avoid
· Leaning backward as you come to the top of the circle.

1 Stand upright, keeping your neck, shoulders, and torso straight.

2 Raise both arms above your head and clasp your hands together, palms facing upward.

3 Keeping your elbows straight, reach to the side to begin tracing a circular pattern with your torso.

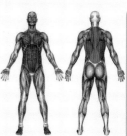

4 Lean forward and then to the opposite side as you slowly trace a full circle.

5 Return to the starting position, and then repeat the sequence 3 times in each direction.

Level
· Beginner

Duration
· 1–2 minutes

Benefits
· Helps correct bad posture
· Mobilizes spine

Caution
· Back issues
· Shoulder pain

Annotation Key
* indicates deep muscles

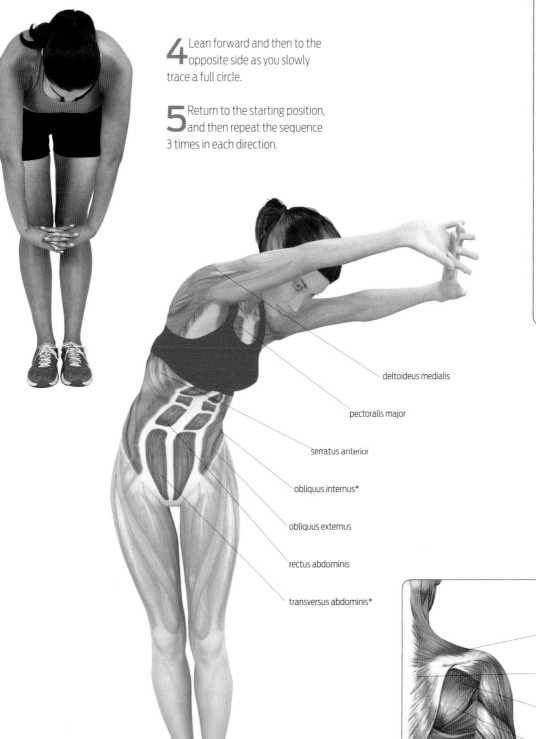

deltoideus medialis

pectoralis major

serratus anterior

obliquus internus*

obliquus externus

rectus abdominis

transversus abdominis*

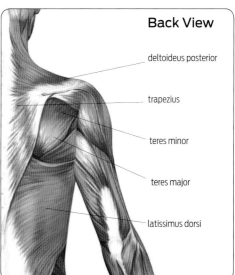

Back View

deltoideus posterior

trapezius

teres minor

teres major

latissimus dorsi

Child's Pose

Use Child's Pose to relax, stretch the back, and release the hips. In the Child's Pose, you will feel a gentle stretch in the lower body from the lower back to the ankles. It is appropriate for everyone, from beginners through advanced exercisers.

1 Kneel on a mat with your hips aligned over your knees.

2 Bring your feet together so that your big toes are touching. Sit back slowly until you are resting your buttocks on your heels.

3 Lower your chest onto your thighs as you extend your hands in front of your head, elongating your neck and spine as you stretch your tailbone toward the mat.

4 Place your forehead on the mat, and hold this position for 30 seconds to 3 minutes.

Correct form
- Round your back to create a dome shape.

Avoid
- Rushing the pose. It can take a few minutes to allow your body to deepen into the full stretch.

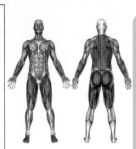

Back View

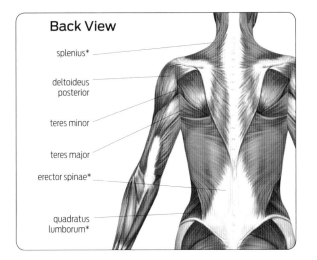

splenius*

deltoideus posterior

teres minor

teres major

erector spinae*

quadratus lumborum*

Level
· Beginner

Duration
· ½–3 minutes

Benefits
· Stretches and relaxes the back and upper body

Caution
· Lower-back or knee pain

Annotation Key
* indicates deep muscles

trapezius

rhomboideus*

deltoideus anterior

brachialis

latissimus dorsi

serratus anterior

biceps brachii

gluteus maximus

extensor carpi radialis

vastus lateralis

flexor digitorum*

triceps brachii

Contents

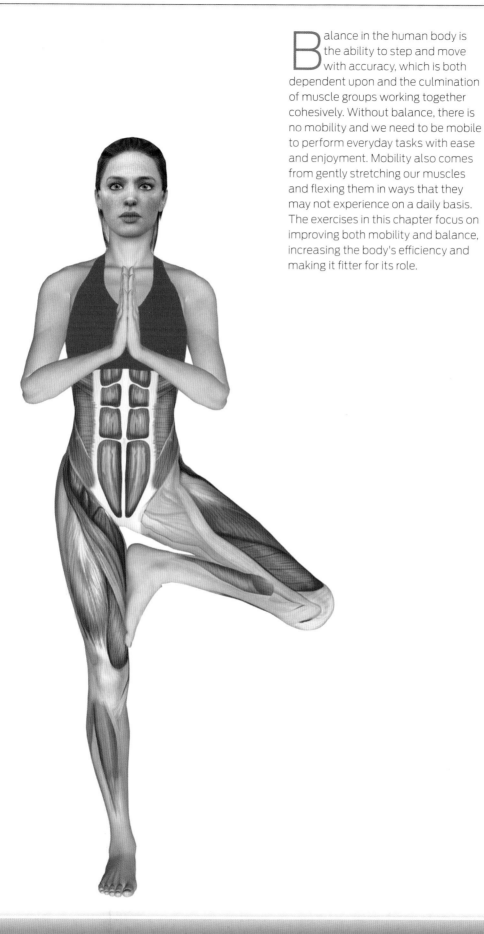

Balance in the human body is the ability to step and move with accuracy, which is both dependent upon and the culmination of muscle groups working together cohesively. Without balance, there is no mobility and we need to be mobile to perform everyday tasks with ease and enjoyment. Mobility also comes from gently stretching our muscles and flexing them in ways that they may not experience on a daily basis. The exercises in this chapter focus on improving both mobility and balance, increasing the body's efficiency and making it fitter for its role.

Mobility & Balance

Thread the Needle

This particular movement pattern is not something we routinely perform in our daily lives. Nevertheless, it is one of a number of exercises that returns the shoulder joints and muscles to normality.

Correct form
· Rotate evenly throughout.

Avoid
· Speeding through the exercise without completing the full range of motion.

1 Begin on all fours with your back flat and your breathing relaxed.

2 Reach one arm underneath your chest. As you do so start to bend your supporting arm to complete the reach through your body.

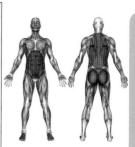

Level
· Intermediate

Duration
· 2–4 minutes

Benefits
· Improves back and shoulder mobility

Caution ⚠
· Lower-back pain
· Wrist or elbow pain
· Shoulder problems

3 Maintain your balance while rotating, until your forearm rests on the floor. Hold the stretch for 1 to 2 minutes, and then repeat on the other side.

Annotation Key
* indicates deep muscles

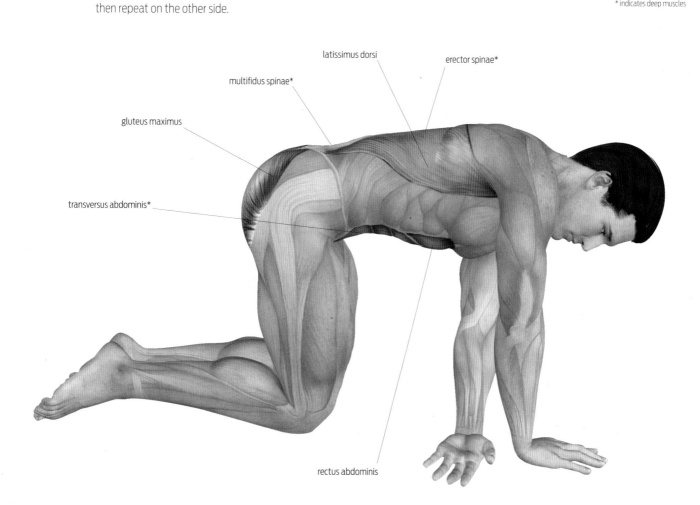

latissimus dorsi

erector spinae*

multifidus spinae*

gluteus maximus

transversus abdominis*

rectus abdominis

Downward-Facing Dog

This pose increases strength and flexibility around the shoulders. It strengthens the entire back and shoulder girdle (the collarbone and shoulder blade), helping to ease back pain. It's a great exercise for invigorating the body and calming the mind after a stressful day, and gently stimulates the nerves.

1 Begin on your hands and knees, with your hands aligned under your shoulders and your knees under your hips.

2 Exhale, and press against the floor, keeping your elbows straight. Lift your seat bones up toward the ceiling and your knees away from the floor. Lengthen your hips away from your ribs to elongate your spine. Hold for 30 seconds to 2 minutes.

Correct form
· Contract your thigh muscles to further lengthen your spine and keep pressure off your shoulders.

Avoid
· Sinking your shoulders into your armpits.
· Creating an arch in your back.

Modification
Harder: Raise one leg toward the ceiling, forming a straight line from head to toe.

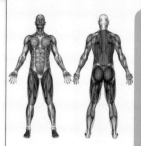

Level
· Beginner

Duration
· 1–3 minutes

Benefits
· Stretches shoulders, glutes, hamstrings, calves, and arches of feet

Caution
· Neck issues
· Arm, wrist, or shoulder problems

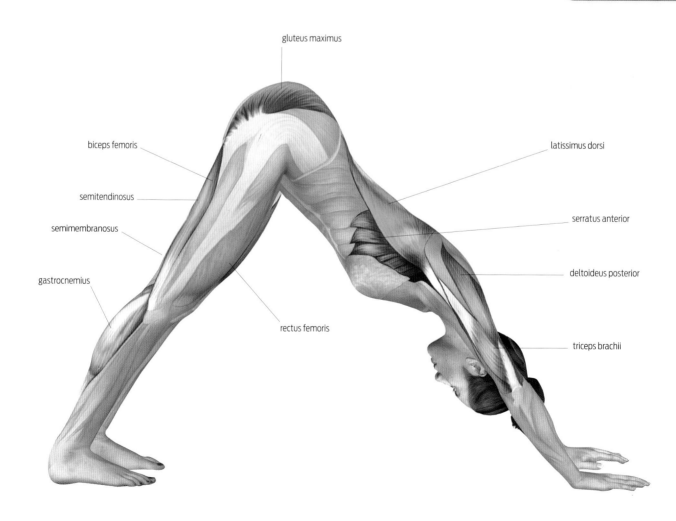

gluteus maximus

biceps femoris

semitendinosus

semimembranosus

gastrocnemius

rectus femoris

latissimus dorsi

serratus anterior

deltoideus posterior

triceps brachii

Upward-Facing Dog

The Upward-Facing Dog pose not only elongates and increases flexibility in your spine, but it's great for opening your chest, throat, shoulders, and the front of your thighs.

Correct form
· Make sure that your wrists are positioned directly below your shoulders so that you don't exert too much pressure on your lower back.

Avoid
· Lifting your shoulders up toward your ears.

1 Lie on the floor with your hands under your shoulders. Lift yourself to a low push-up or low plank, supporting your weight evenly between your hands and feet.

2 Lift your torso upward and face forward.

3 Flip the tops of your feet to the floor and straighten your arms with your shoulders above your wrists.

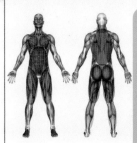

4 Keeping your knees and thighs off the floor, lift your hips and look upward. Hold this position for 10 to 15 seconds.

Level
· Intermediate

Duration
· ½–1 minute

Benefits
· Strengthens the arms, wrists, and abs
· Increases the flexibility of the back

Caution
· Hip or leg issues
· Lower-back pain
· Wrist problems

Annotation Key
* indicates deep muscles

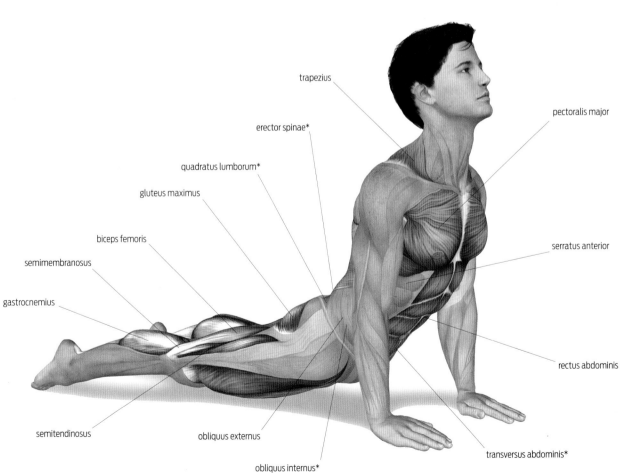

trapezius

erector spinae*

quadratus lumborum*

gluteus maximus

biceps femoris

semimembranosus

gastrocnemius

semitendinosus

obliquus externus

obliquus internus*

transversus abdominis*

rectus abdominis

serratus anterior

pectoralis major

Side Bends

Side Bends are perfect for stretching the serratus, oblique, and intercostal muscles. This exercise can be modified by placing one hand on your hip and one arm overhead (simpler) or by holding a weight or dumbbell overhead (more difficult). Keep within your comfort zone and increase the stretch over time.

1 Stand with your neck, shoulders, and torso straight.

2 Raise both arms above your head and clasp your hands together, palms facing upward.

3 Leaning from the hips, slowly drop your torso to the left.

Correct form
· Maintain an upright posture.

Avoid
· Bending forward or backward at the trunk.

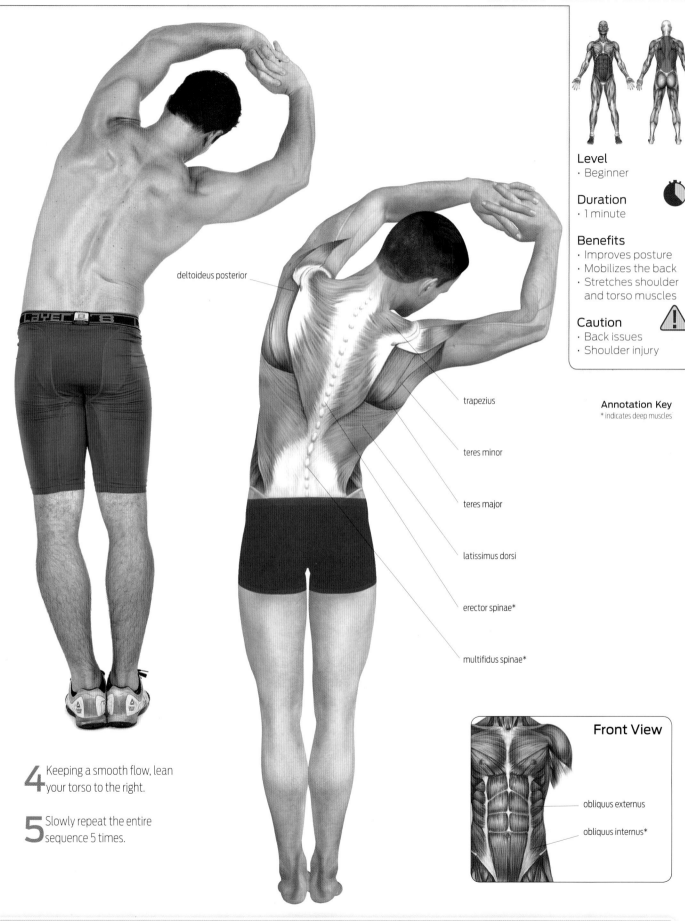

Level
· Beginner

Duration
· 1 minute

Benefits
· Improves posture
· Mobilizes the back
· Stretches shoulder and torso muscles

Caution
· Back issues
· Shoulder injury

Annotation Key
* indicates deep muscles

deltoideus posterior

trapezius

teres minor

teres major

latissimus dorsi

erector spinae*

multifidus spinae*

4 Keeping a smooth flow, lean your torso to the right.

5 Slowly repeat the entire sequence 5 times.

Front View

obliquus externus

obliquus internus*

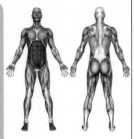

Upward Salute

This exercise targets the shoulders and, to a lesser degree, the chest, neck, biceps, forearms, triceps, lats, middle back, and lower back. It is a good back stretch.

Level
· Beginner

Duration
· ½–1 minute

Benefits
· Alleviates backache
· Improves posture

Caution
· Shoulder issues
· Back problems

Annotation Key
* indicates deep muscles

1 Stand tall with your arms at your sides. Feel that your spine is straight.

2 Inhale, and raise your arms out to your sides, elongating your torso and continuing to raise your arms until they are directly above your head.

3 Lengthen your arms with your palms facing each other, and hold for 10 to 30 seconds.

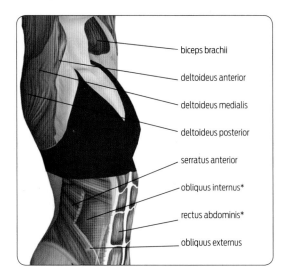

- biceps brachii
- deltoideus anterior
- deltoideus medialis
- deltoideus posterior
- serratus anterior
- obliquus internus*
- rectus abdominis*
- obliquus externus

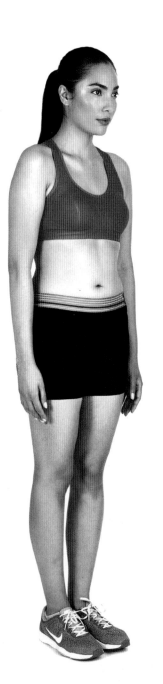

Correct form
· Keep your shoulders aligned over your hips and your hips over your heels.

Avoid
· Jutting your rib cage out of your chest.

Tree Pose

Stretching the thighs, groins, torso, and shoulders, the Tree Pose is excellent for toning the leg and abdominal muscles. It improves balance and is also therapeutic for sciatica.

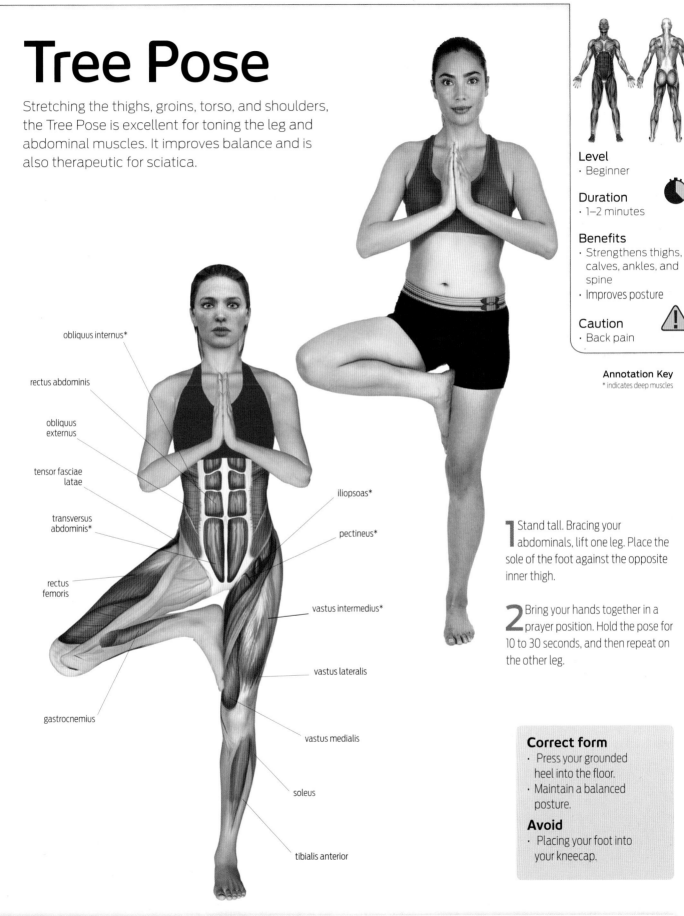

Level
· Beginner

Duration
· 1–2 minutes

Benefits
· Strengthens thighs, calves, ankles, and spine
· Improves posture

Caution
· Back pain

Annotation Key
* indicates deep muscles

obliquus internus*

rectus abdominis

obliquus externus

tensor fasciae latae

transversus abdominis*

rectus femoris

gastrocnemius

iliopsoas*

pectineus*

vastus intermedius*

vastus lateralis

vastus medialis

soleus

tibialis anterior

1 Stand tall. Bracing your abdominals, lift one leg. Place the sole of the foot against the opposite inner thigh.

2 Bring your hands together in a prayer position. Hold the pose for 10 to 30 seconds, and then repeat on the other leg.

Correct form
· Press your grounded heel into the floor.
· Maintain a balanced posture.

Avoid
· Placing your foot into your kneecap.

Balance Walk

This simple walking exercise can be done anywhere and will help to improve your posture, balance, and mobility. It brings mindfulness to an everyday activity. The key is to consider each step, hold it for a second or two, and then move on.

1 Raise your arms out to your sides at shoulder height. Begin walking.

2 Move slowly and deliberately, lifting your front leg high and stretching your back foot out behind you before bringing it forward.

3 As you lift your back leg out behind you, pause for a second or two before bringing it forward.

Correct form
· Imagine you are walking on an invisible tightrope.

Avoid
· Slouching or rounding your back.

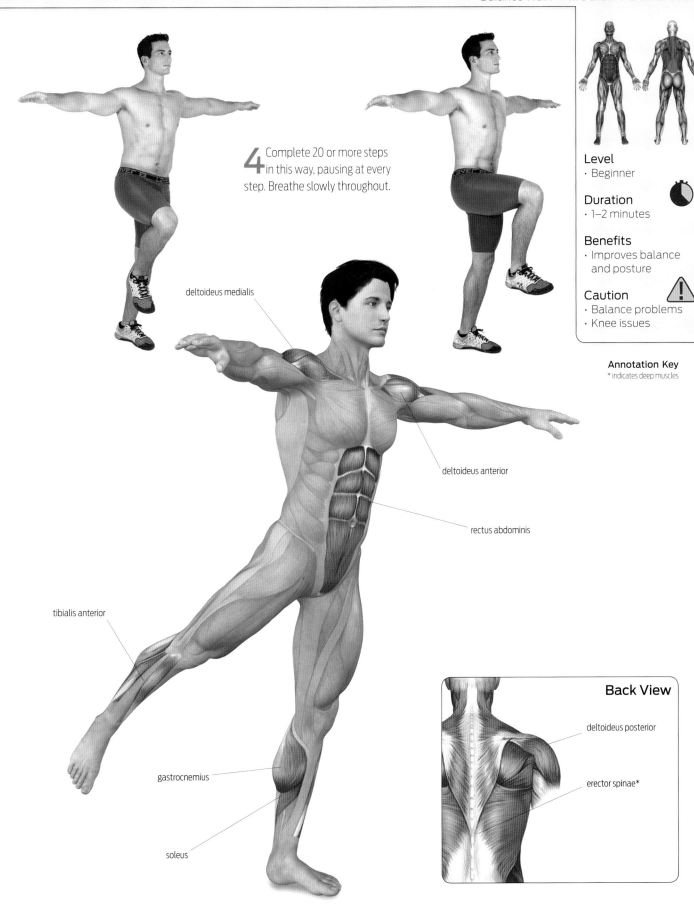

4 Complete 20 or more steps in this way, pausing at every step. Breathe slowly throughout.

Level
· Beginner

Duration
· 1–2 minutes

Benefits
· Improves balance and posture

Caution
· Balance problems
· Knee issues

Annotation Key
* indicates deep muscles

deltoideus medialis

deltoideus anterior

rectus abdominis

tibialis anterior

gastrocnemius

soleus

Back View

deltoideus posterior

erector spinae*

Contents

Body-Weight Exercises

Today's demanding lifestyles make it difficult for many of us to find the time to get to the gym. For this reason, body-weight workouts, which can be performed almost anywhere, are rapidly becoming the norm. These exercises also offer myriad benefits too good to ignore. Not only do they increase muscle strength, they also improve cardio output. Another major benefit is their effect on functional strength—the strength we need to go about our daily lives in good health and comfort. Then there is the underlying beauty of body-weight exercises—something that makes them suitable for everyone: they can easily be adjusted to your level of fitness and you can increase the challenge as you become fitter.

Step Down

This is a knee-strengthening exercise. It is a challenging movement that will put a lot of strain on your muscles. It can be modified in two ways: changing the height of the step-up box, or changing the speed of the motion. The slower the motion, the more difficult the exercise; the higher the box, the more difficult the exercise.

1 Standing up straight on a firm block or step, plant your left foot close to the edge, and allow the right foot to hang off the side. Flex the toes of your right foot.

2 Lift your arms out in front of you for balance, keeping them parallel to the floor. Lower your torso as you bend at your hips and knees, dropping your right leg toward the floor.

3 Without rotating your torso or knee, press upward through your left leg to return to the starting position. Repeat up to 15 times. Rest. Do a second set with the same leg. Switch legs and repeat.

Correct form
· Bend your knee to align with your toes—your knee should not rotate inward.

Avoid
· Placing weight on the foot that is being lowered to the floor—allow only a touch.

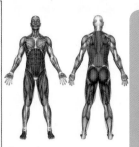

Level
· Intermediate

Duration
· 1½–2 minutes

Benefits
· Strengthens the pelvic and knee stabilizers
· Core strength

Caution
· Lower-back pain
· Knee pain
· Hip problems

Annotation Key
* indicates deep muscles

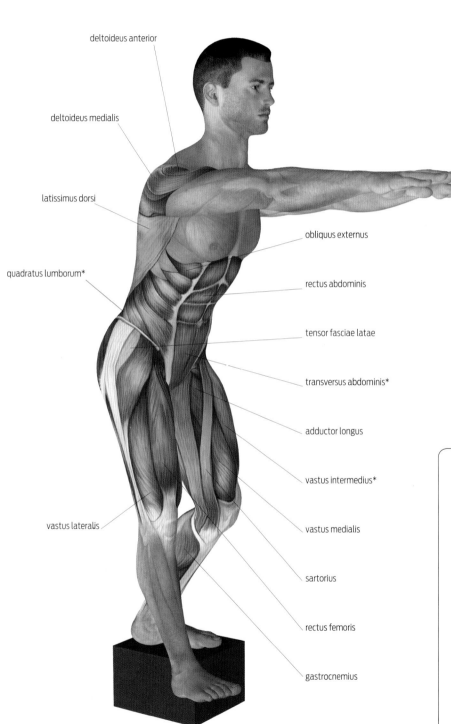

deltoideus anterior

deltoideus medialis

latissimus dorsi

quadratus lumborum*

vastus lateralis

obliquus externus

rectus abdominis

tensor fasciae latae

transversus abdominis*

adductor longus

vastus intermedius*

vastus medialis

sartorius

rectus femoris

gastrocnemius

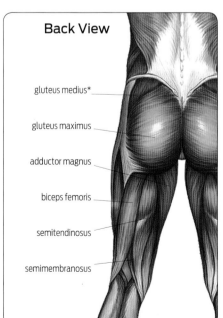

Back View

gluteus medius*

gluteus maximus

adductor magnus

biceps femoris

semitendinosus

semimembranosus

Sit-Up

The Sit-Up is to the abdominals what the bench press is to the pectorals. This iconic movement must be one of the most widely and regularly used exercises worldwide and for good reason: it's perfect for the rectus abdominis. The Crunch (see pages 56–57) is similar but focuses on fewer muscle groups.

Correct form
· Lead from your belly button.

Avoid
· Overusing your neck to rise up or lower yourself back down.

1 Begin by lying on your back with your legs bent and your hands behind your head.

2 Start by pushing through your heels for support and raising your trunk off the ground, contracting your abdominals while lifting your torso up toward your knees.

3 Raise as far as you can without forcing the movement or twisting your body to do so. Lower slowly and under control. Repeat for 20 repetitions.

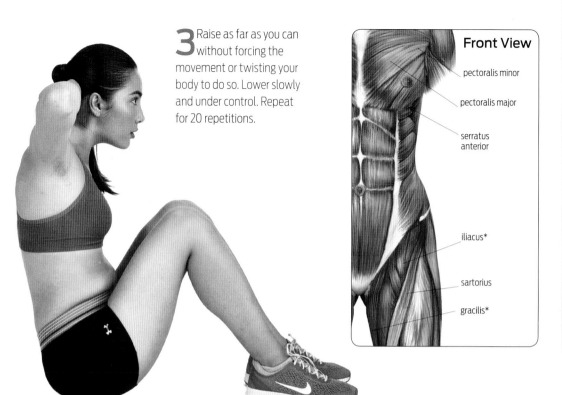

Front View

- pectoralis minor
- pectoralis major
- serratus anterior
- iliacus*
- sartorius
- gracilis*

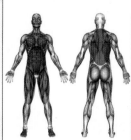

Level
· Beginner

Duration
· 2–3 minutes

Benefits
· Strengthens key core muscles
· Tones the abs

Caution
· Neck issues
· Lower-back problems

Annotation Key
* indicates deep muscles

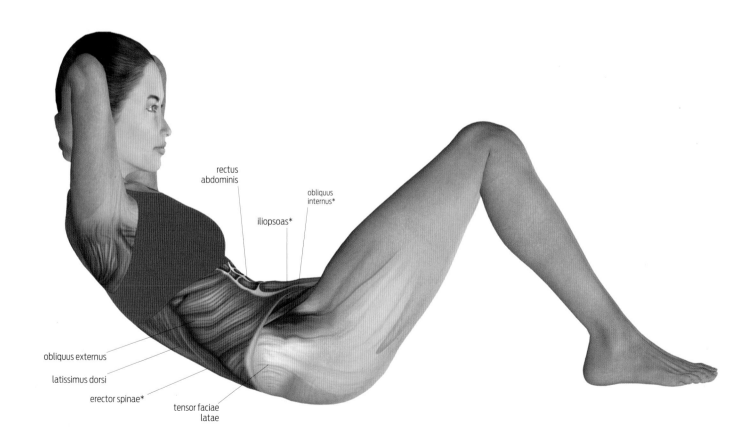

- rectus abdominis
- obliquus internus*
- iliopsoas*
- obliquus externus
- latissimus dorsi
- erector spinae*
- tensor faciae latae

Double-Leg Ab Press

Pressing as hard as you can against your quadriceps is a great workout for your core muscles. If this is too difficult, the exercise can be modified by pressing on one leg at a time.

Correct form
· Keep your feet flexed and your knees pressed together.
· Press equally with both hands.

Avoid
· Holding your breath.
· Twisting your shoulders.

1 Lie on your back with your knees and feet lifted in tabletop position, your thighs making a 90-degree angle with your upper body. Place your hands on the front of your knees, your fingers facing upward, a palm on each leg.

2 Flex your feet and, keeping your elbows bent and pulled into your sides, press your hands into your knees. Create resistance by pushing back against your hands with your knees.

3 Lift your shoulders off the floor. Hold for up to a minute. Repeat 5 times.

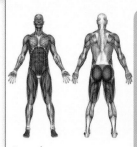

Modification

Easier: Beginners can plant their feet against a hard surface for extra support.

Front View

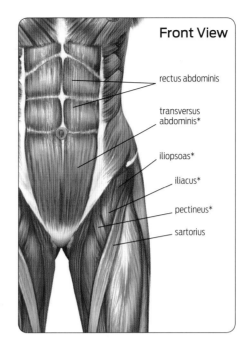

rectus abdominis

transversus abdominis*

iliopsoas*

iliacus*

pectineus*

sartorius

Level
· Beginner

Duration
· 3–5 minutes

Benefits
· Strengthens core, hip flexors, and triceps

Caution
· Shoulder issues
· Neck issues
· Lower-back pain

Annotation Key
* indicates deep muscles

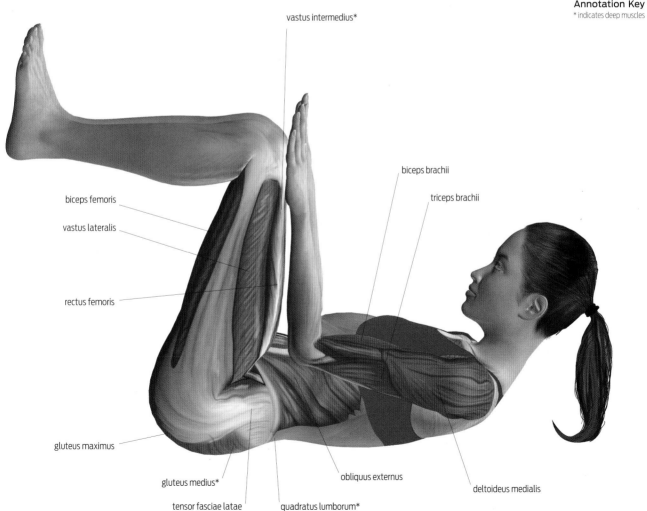

vastus intermedius*

biceps femoris

vastus lateralis

rectus femoris

gluteus maximus

gluteus medius*

tensor fasciae latae

quadratus lumborum*

obliquus externus

biceps brachii

triceps brachii

deltoideus medialis

Lemon Squeezer

If you need to take your abdominal workout to a higher intensity than is offered by a sit-up, try a Lemon Squeezer, in which you visualize an imaginary lemon on your stomach that you squeeze by raising your legs and torso off the ground while contracting your ab muscles.

1 Lie flat on the floor with your arms straight down by your side.

2 Lift your legs, head, neck, and shoulders slightly off the floor, being careful not to arch your lower back. Your arms should be raised and parallel to the floor, hands stretched out.

3 Squeeze your abs to bring your torso up off the ground. Pause at the top of the movement, and then lower yourself almost to the starting position. Repeat the motion without completely lying down on the mat. Do two sets of 15 repetitions.

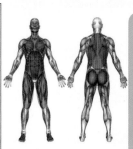

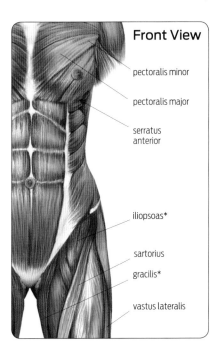

Front View

- pectoralis minor
- pectoralis major
- serratus anterior
- iliopsoas*
- sartorius
- gracilis*
- vastus lateralis

Level
- Intermediate

Duration
- ½–1 minute

Benefits
- Increases core strength

Caution
- Shoulder issues
- Neck issues
- Lower-back pain

Annotation Key
* indicates deep muscles

Correct form
- The chin remains tucked.
- Keep your thigh muscles firm throughout the exercise.

Avoid
- Allowing your shoulders to lift up toward your ears.

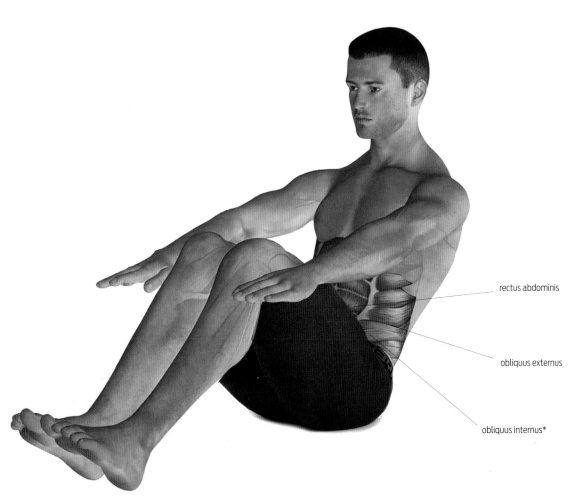

- rectus abdominis
- obliquus externus
- obliquus internus*

Crunch

A highly effective abdominal isolator, the Crunch is similar to the Sit-Up (pages 50–51) but is shorter in range of motion. It places more tension on the muscles, with less help from ancillary tissues. Its difficulty can be increased by lying on a declined bench, placing a weight on the chest, or holding a weight behind the head. Crunches can also be performed with your hands crossed over your chest.

Correct form
· Maintain a precise and short range of motion.

Avoid
· Using the neck.
· Bouncy and speedy repetitions.

1 Begin by lying down on your back, your legs bent and your palms placed behind your head with your elbows flared outward.

2 Raise your head and shoulders off the ground while contracting your trunk toward your waist.

3 Keeping the base of your spine to the floor, lower and repeat for up to 40 repetitions.

Modification

Harder: Begin with your arms stretched above your head. Without lifting your legs, bring your arms and torso upward in a controlled movement. Continue to curl forward until you can grasp your feet, or as nearly as possible. Uncurling slowly and under control, return to the start position.

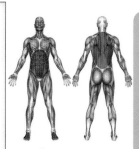

Level
· Beginner

Duration
· 1–2 minutes

Benefits
· Strengthens core muscles without pressurizing lower spine

Caution

· Back issues
· Shoulder injury

Annotation Key
* indicates deep muscles

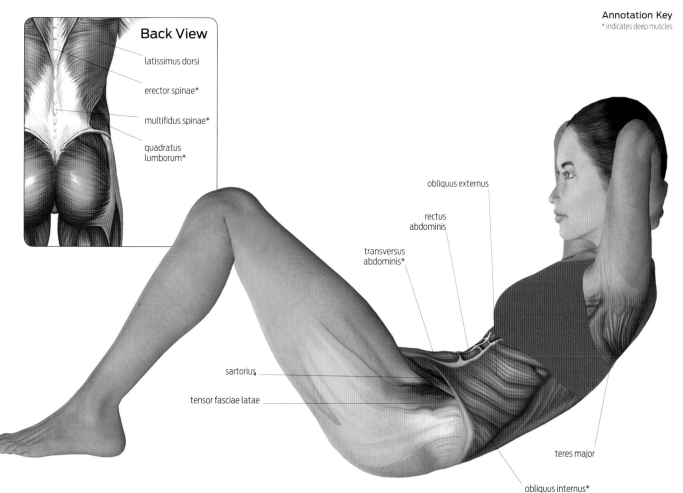

Back View
latissimus dorsi

erector spinae*

multifidus spinae*

quadratus lumborum*

obliquus externus

rectus abdominis

transversus abdominis*

sartorius

tensor fasciae latae

teres major

obliquus internus*

Chair Abdominal Crunch

Chair workouts are great for anyone who spends a lot of time at a desk, and for people with poor balance or limited mobility who can benefit from the support a chair offers. Because your abdominals are a group of smaller, linked muscles, they benefit from daily workouts, and rarely require a day of rest between.

Correct form
· Your spine is neutral as you progress through the motion.
· Your knees align over your ankles.
· Your body remains close to the chair.

Avoid
· Allowing your shoulders to lift up toward your ears.

1 Sit on a chair with your hands grasping the sides of the seat and your arms straight.

2 Move your torso forward and if possible lift your buttocks slightly off the chair. Your hips and knees should be bent to form 90-degree angles.

3 In one movement, tuck your tailbone toward the front of the chair and bend your knees toward your chest. As you bend your knees, slightly bend your elbows as well.

4 Keeping your head in a neutral position, extend your elbows and press through your shoulders into the chair and lower your legs to return to the starting position. Repeat 15 times for two sets.

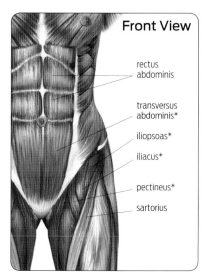

Front View

- rectus abdominis
- transversus abdominis*
- iliopsoas*
- iliacus*
- pectineus*
- sartorius

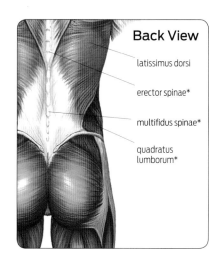

Back View

- latissimus dorsi
- erector spinae*
- multifidus spinae*
- quadratus lumborum*

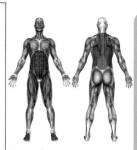

Level
· Advanced

Duration
· 2–3 minutes

Benefits
· Increases upper body strength
· Improves shoulder stability

Caution
· Shoulder issues
· Lower-back pain

Annotation Key
* indicates deep muscles

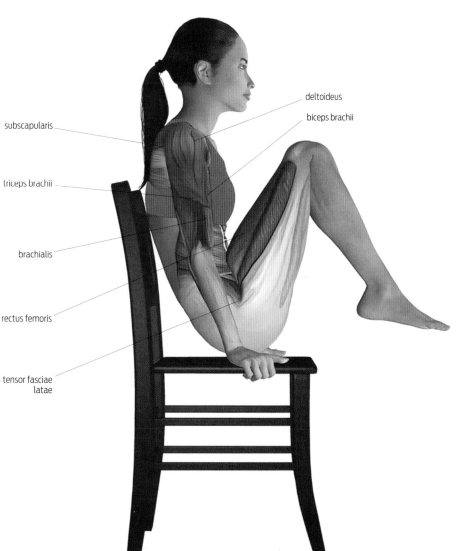

- subscapularis
- triceps brachii
- brachialis
- rectus femoris
- tensor fasciae latae
- deltoideus
- biceps brachii

Abdominal Hip Lift

The Abdominal Hip Lift strengthens the rectus abdominis (the muscle between the ribs and hips) and the obliques. Work up to 2 sets of 10 to 20 repetitions, with a short break between. An alternative is to cross the feet and change the front leg between sets.

1 Lie down with your legs in the air, knees straight. Place your arms on the floor, straight by your sides.

2 Pinching your legs together and squeezing your buttocks, press into the back of your arms to lift your hips upward. This is a small movement.

3 Slowly return your hips to the floor. Repeat 10–20 times. Focus on your abs as you do the lift.

Correct form
· Keep your legs as straight as possible throughout the exercise.

Avoid
· Using momentum, and bringing the lower back too much into play.

Modification
Easier: This exercise can be modified by bending the legs to reduce the stress on the abdominals.

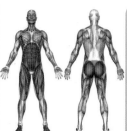

Back View

quadratus lumborum*

gluteus medius*

piriformis*

gluteus maximus

Modification

Harder: This move works from the upper body, rather than the hips. Keep your hips down and raise your arms toward the ceiling.

Level
· Intermediate

Duration
· 1–2 minutes

Benefits
· Improves core strength

Caution
· Shoulder issues
· Hip issues
· Lower-back pain

Annotation Key
* indicates deep muscles

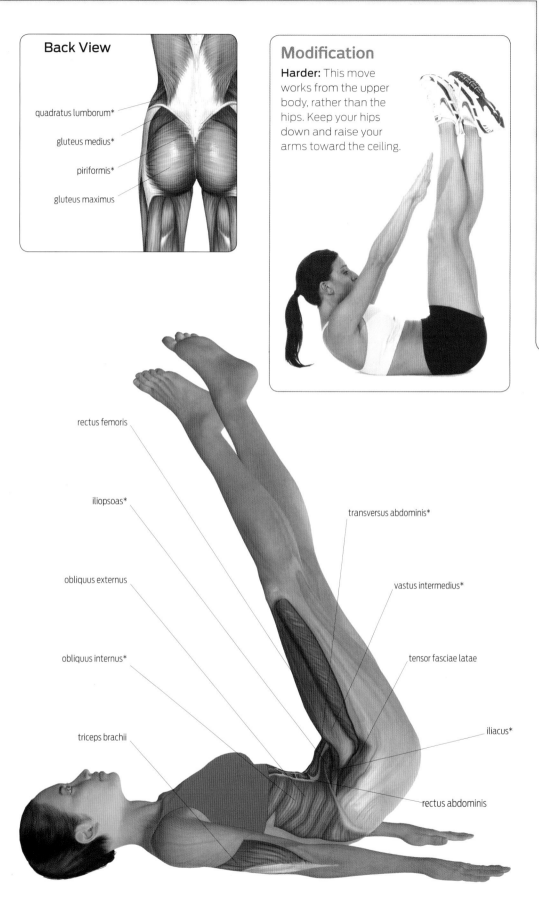

rectus femoris

iliopsoas*

obliquus externus

obliquus internus*

triceps brachii

transversus abdominis*

vastus intermedius*

tensor fasciae latae

iliacus*

rectus abdominis

Kneeling Side Kick

The Kneeling Side Kick helps exercise your buttocks. It tones and strengthens your seat muscles, especially the gluteus medius (the smallest of the glute muscles). Strong glutes help you to produce elegant, healthy, and balanced movement patterns.

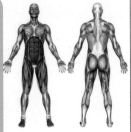

Level
· Advanced

Duration
· 2—3 minutes

Benefits
· Tones glutes and strengthens core

Caution
· Shoulder issues
· Arm or wrist issues
· Any back pain

Annotation Key
* indicates deep muscles

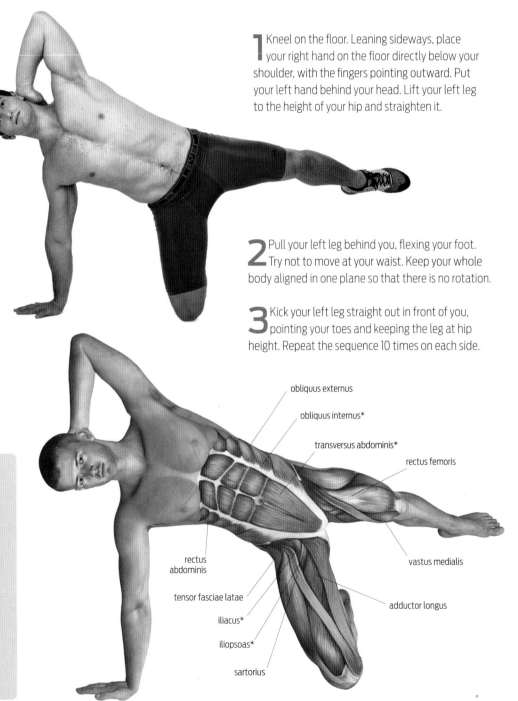

1 Kneel on the floor. Leaning sideways, place your right hand on the floor directly below your shoulder, with the fingers pointing outward. Put your left hand behind your head. Lift your left leg to the height of your hip and straighten it.

2 Pull your left leg behind you, flexing your foot. Try not to move at your waist. Keep your whole body aligned in one plane so that there is no rotation.

3 Kick your left leg straight out in front of you, pointing your toes and keeping the leg at hip height. Repeat the sequence 10 times on each side.

obliquus externus

obliquus internus*

transversus abdominis*

rectus femoris

rectus abdominis

vastus medialis

tensor fasciae latae

adductor longus

iliacus*

iliopsoas*

sartorius

Correct form
· Bear your weight on the palm of your hand to help maintain balance.
· Your neck remains long and relaxed.
· Your body aligns so that your shoulders, hips, and legs line up to better activate deep muscles.

Avoid
· Wobbling when moving the leg—instead, make the movement smaller.

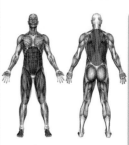

Thigh Rock-Back

The Thigh Rock-Back is a simple but effective exercise that improves abdominal and thigh strength. Regular practice will also tone your glutes.

1 Begin in a kneeling position, with a straight back and your arms at your sides.

2 Lean back while keeping your body in a straight line and your abdominals contracted.

3 While still leaning back, flex your glute muscles, then slowly return to the starting position. Complete 10 repetitions.

Level
· Intermediate

Duration
· 1–2 minutes

Benefits
· Tones thighs, torso, and glutes

Caution
· Back pain
· Knee issues
· Pelvic problems

Annotation Key
* indicates deep muscles

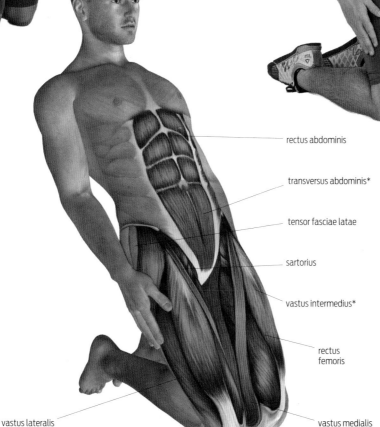

- rectus abdominis
- transversus abdominis*
- tensor fasciae latae
- sartorius
- vastus intermedius*
- rectus femoris
- vastus lateralis
- vastus medialis

Correct form
· Maintain a straight line with your torso

Avoid
· Leaning back too far.

V-Up

V-Ups are a challenging means of isolating the rectus abdominis through an entire range of motion, which makes them an effective core-strengthening exercise. They also mobilize the spine. Precision is important to ensure the correct muscles are used.

Correct form
· Articulate through the spine on the way up and on the way down.

Avoid
· Shortening and stiffening your neck, so minimizing tension in your upper spine.

1 Begin by lying on your back, arms by your sides.

2 Simultaneously raise both legs and lift your torso, reaching your arms forward until they are nearly touching your feet.

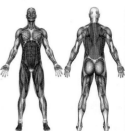

Level
· Intermediate

Duration
· 2—3 minutes

Benefits
· Strengthens the abdominals
· Increases spinal flexibility

Caution
· Lower-back pain
· Hip issues

Annotation Key
*indicates deep muscles

3 Maintain a flat back and try to form a perfect V shape with your torso and legs. Lower and repeat for 25 repetitions.

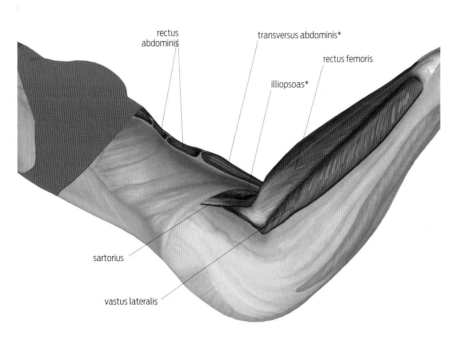

rectus abdominis

transversus abdominis*

rectus femoris

illiopsoas*

sartorius

vastus lateralis

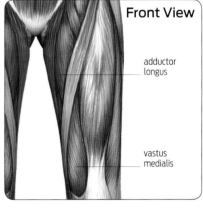

Front View

adductor longus

vastus medialis

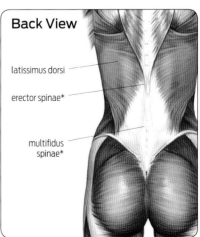

Back View

latissimus dorsi

erector spinae*

multifidus spinae*

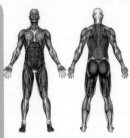

Bridge

This classic yoga and Pilates exercise functions as a core strengthener and a back stretch, while also enhancing core stability and working the glutes. To perform it correctly, you need to keep your body aligned. Being mindful of the muscles you use will increase its effectiveness.

Level
· Beginner

Duration
· 1½–2 minutes

Benefits
· Core strength and control

Caution
· Shoulder issues
· Arm issues
· Any back pain

Annotation Key
*indicates deep muscles

1 Begin on your back with your legs bent, your feet flat on the ground, and your arms extended on the floor, parallel to your body.

2 Push through your heels, raising your pelvis until your torso and thighs are aligned. Hold for 30 seconds, then lower yourself back down. Perform 3 repetitions.

Correct form
· Push through your heels, not your toes.

Avoid
· Overextending your abs past your thighs in the finished position.

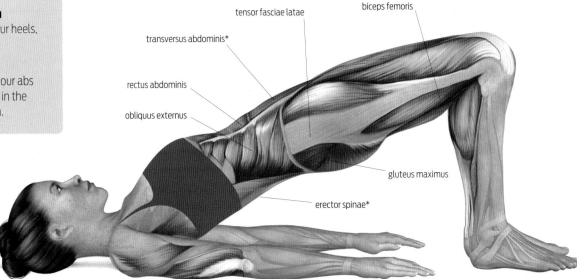

tensor fasciae latae

biceps femoris

transversus abdominis*

rectus abdominis

obliquus externus

gluteus maximus

erector spinae*

Scissors

Improving core stability while increasing abdominal strength and endurance, the Scissors is also a good stretch for the hamstrings. Done correctly, it will help mobilize the shoulders and upper arms.

1 Lie on the floor with your arms by your sides and your legs raised in a tabletop position.

2 Inhale, drawing in your abdominals. Reach your legs straight up, and lift your head and shoulders off the floor. Hold the position while lengthening your legs.

3 Stretching your left leg away from your body, raise your right leg. Hold your right calf with your hands, pulsing twice while keeping your shoulders relaxed.

4 Repeat the motion with your left leg raised and your right leg stretched away. Continue, alternating legs and doing 5–8 reps on each side.

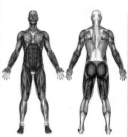

Level
· Intermediate

Duration
· 1–2 minutes

Benefits
· Core stability and control

Caution
· Back pain
· Shoulder issues
· Tight hamstrings

Annotation Key
indicates deep muscles

Correct form
· Keep your pelvis stabilized and your spine straight.

Avoid
· Overextending your raised leg.

Modification

Harder: This exercise can be modified by performing 5-8 repetitions on one leg before switching to the other.

rectus femoris

sartorius

rectus abdominis

vastus lateralis

Alternating Sit-Up

The Alternating Sit-Up is an advanced variant on the classic Sit-Up (see pages 50–51). In addition to increasing the strength of the rectus abdominis and other core muscles, it focuses more intensely on the obliques. As such it is a key foundation exercise for abdominal and core strength.

Correct form
· Lead from your belly button, keeping your back straight.

Avoid
· Overusing your neck or arching your back to lift your torso.

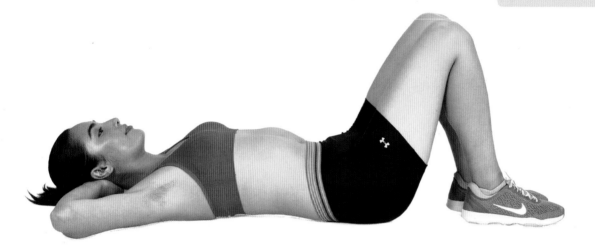

1 Lie on your back with your legs slightly bent and your hands behind your head, elbows flat on the floor.

2 Push through your heels for support and raise your trunk off the ground by contracting your abdominal muscles.

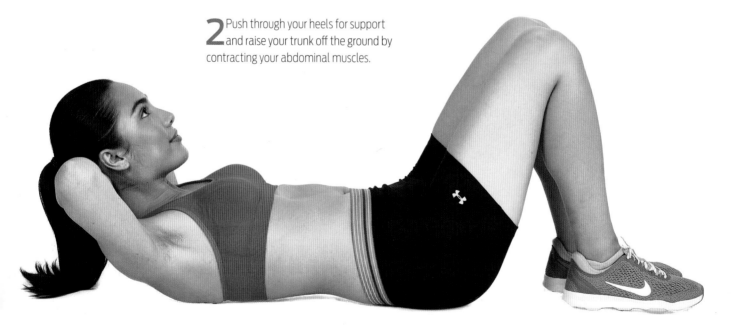

Back View

- subscapularis*
- teres major
- latissimus dorsi
- erector spinae*
- quadratus lumborum*
- multifidus spinae*

3 As you rise, rotate to the right so your left elbow touches your right knee, and contract your oblique muscles.

4 Lower your back to the floor. Repeat the sit-up, this time rotating to the other side. Perform 15 repetitions each side.

Level
- Intermediate

Duration
- 2–3 minutes

Benefits
- Strengthens the core
- Increases mobility in the spine

Caution
- Hip issues
- Lower-back pain
- Shoulder pain

Annotation Key
* indicates deep muscles

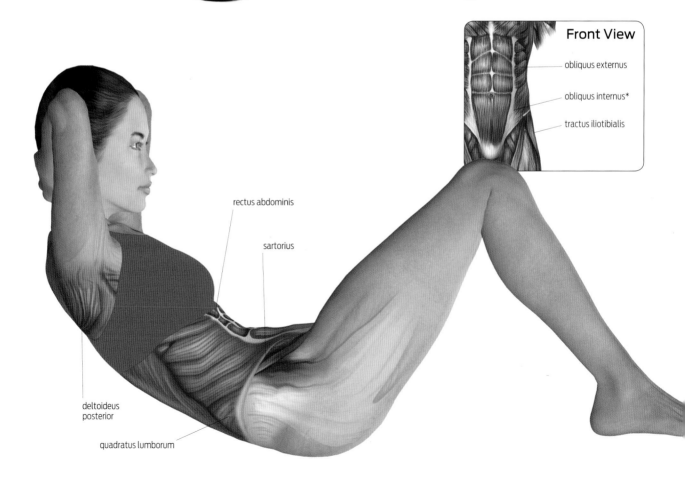

Front View

- obliquus externus
- obliquus internus*
- tractus iliotibialis

- rectus abdominis
- sartorius
- deltoideus posterior
- quadratus lumborum

Bridge with Leg Lift

An excellent addition to the classic Bridge (see page 66), this exercise works the abdominals, back, and buttocks. It also improves balance. It can be simplified by decreasing the range of motion—just raise your foot slightly off the floor. If necessary, prop yourself up with your hands beneath your hips once in the bridge position.

Correct form
· Keep your pelvis level as you lift.
· Ensure your shoulders remain relaxed.

Avoid
· Excessively bending the knee. Bring it only so far to the chest as your current flexibility levels will allow.

1 Lie on the floor, your arms by your sides and fingers lengthened toward your feet. Your knees should be bent, with your feet flat on the floor.

2 Lift your hips and spine off the floor, creating one long line from your knees to your shoulders. Keep your weight over your feet.

3 Keeping your legs bent, bring your left knee toward your chest then lower it until your toe touches the mat. Bring your left knee toward your chest again. Repeat 4–5 times. Lower leg to the floor.

4 Repeat the exercise with your right leg. Repeat 4–5 times.

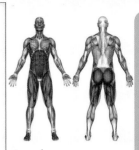

Level
· Beginner

Duration

· 2–4 minutes

Benefits
· Strengthens glutes and abdominals

Caution

· Knee or hip issues
· Lower-back pain

Annotation Key
* indicates deep muscles

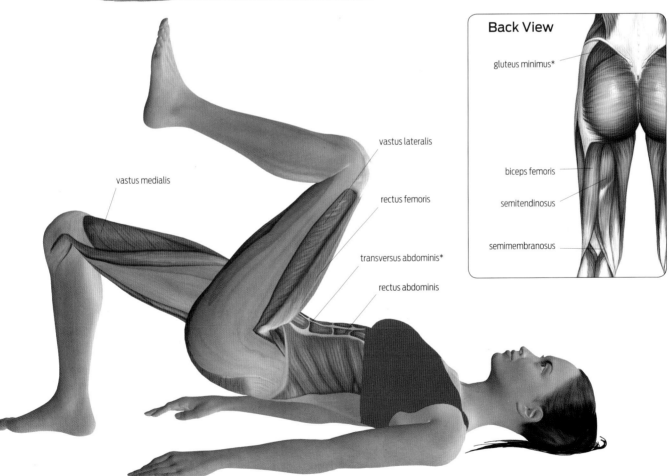

vastus lateralis

vastus medialis

rectus femoris

transversus abdominis*

rectus abdominis

Back View

gluteus minimus*

biceps femoris

semitendinosus

semimembranosus

Leg Raises

Leg Raises are a simple exercise, good for strengthening the area commonly called the "lower abdominals"—although this label is incorrect, as the rectus abdominis is one muscle and not sectionalized. The exercise is particularly felt below the navel.

Correct form
· Keep your upper body braced.
· Maintain a controlled lowering.
· Use a precise range of motion.

Avoid
· Letting your legs touch the ground.
· Stressing your lower back.
· Swinging with momentum.

1 Begin by lying on your back with your arms at your sides and your legs outstretched with toes pointed and your heels elevated just off the ground.

2 Raise both legs until they are nearly at a 90-degree angle to the ground.

3 Lower your legs to just short of the ground and repeat for 25 repetitions.

Modification

Easier: This exercise can be modified by bending the legs to reduce the stress on the abdominals.

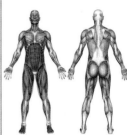

Level
· Intermediate

Duration
· 2–3 minutes

Benefits
· Improves core strength and support.

Caution
· Neck issues
· Back or hip pain

Annotation Key
* indicates deep muscles

iliopsoas*

transversus abdominis*

sartorius

vastus intermedius*

obliquus externus

rectus femoris

obliquus internus*

rectus abdominis

vastus lateralis

Knee-Pull Plank

The aim of the Knee-Pull Plank is to build core strength. When you do it, your abdominals will get a good workout, and the exercise also helps improve balance and build endurance in your upper body. Keep the movements slow and precise.

Correct form
· Keep your body in a straight line throughout the exercise.

Avoid
· Bending the knee of the supporting leg.

1 Begin by assuming a standard plank position.

2 Draw your right knee into your chest while leaning forward and flexing your foot. Your left foot should be up on its toes.

3 Extend your left leg through the heel and rock your body back, shifting your weight into your left foot.

4 Keeping your spine aligned, straighten and raise your right leg toward the ceiling. Repeat the entire exercise 10 times per leg.

Modification

Easier: This exercise can be made easier by using a wall to help support the raised leg.

Level
· Advanced

Duration
· 2–3 minutes

Benefits
· Improves core stabilization and flexibility

Caution
· Lower-back issues
· Shoulder pain
· Wrist pain

Annotation Key
* indicates deep muscles

Back View

quadratus lumborum*
gluteus medius*
gluteus minimus*
piriformis*
gluteus maximus
gemellus superior*
semitendinosus

vastus lateralis

rectus femoris

gracilis*

sartorius

vastus medialis

semimembranosus

gastrocnemius

peroneus

tibialis posterior*

biceps femoris

tensor fasciae latae

transversus abdominis*

latissimus dorsi

obliquus externus

teres major

deltoideus medialis

adductor longus

adductor magnus

rectus abdominis

vastus intermedius*

tibialis anterior

soleus

Front Plank

The Front Plank, or Reverse Plank, is often overlooked, but is very useful since it isolates and strengthens the gluteus muscles and hamstrings. Done correctly, it engages both the abdominals and the lower-back muscles. It can also be used as a rehab exercise to improve core and spinal stabilization.

1 Sit with your legs extended in front of you and your arms directly behind you, with your fingers pointing straight ahead.

2 Push through your palms and raise your hips and glutes off the ground until your body forms a straight line from the shoulders to the feet.

Correct form
· Keep your pelvis elevated for the duration of the exercise.

Avoid
· Letting your shoulders slouch backward.

3 Raise one leg and hold for 30 seconds, then switch legs.

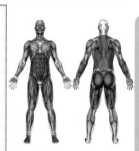

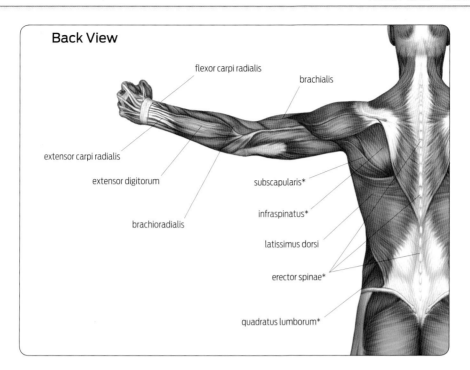

Back View

flexor carpi radialis

brachialis

extensor carpi radialis

extensor digitorum

subscapularis*

brachioradialis

infraspinatus*

latissimus dorsi

erector spinae*

quadratus lumborum*

Level
· Intermediate

Duration
· 2–3 minutes

Benefits
· Stabilizes core and strengthens abdominals

Caution
· Back issues
· Shoulder pain

Annotation Key
* indicates deep muscles

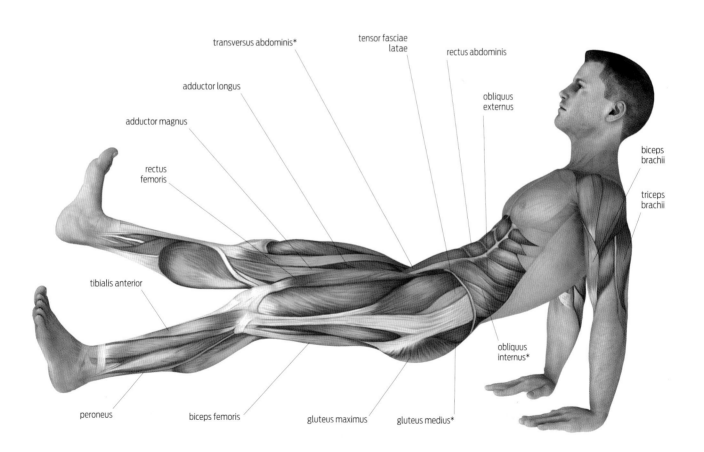

transversus abdominis*

tensor fasciae latae

rectus abdominis

adductor longus

obliquus externus

adductor magnus

rectus femoris

biceps brachii

triceps brachii

tibialis anterior

obliquus internus*

peroneus

biceps femoris

gluteus maximus

gluteus medius*

Side-Bend Plank

The Side-Bend Plank is great for those starting an exercise regimen. Increasing the amount of time spent performing the basic side plank will greatly increase its intensity. You'll be suprised at how a few extra seconds can make this exercise much more difficult!

1 Lie on your right side with one arm supporting your torso, aligning the wrist under your shoulder. Place your left arm on top of your left leg. Your legs should be strongly squeezed together, with legs parallel and feet flexed. Draw your navel toward your spine.

2 Press into the palm of your right hand and lift your hips off the floor, creating a straight line between your heels and head.

3 Hold until failure, then repeat on the other arm.

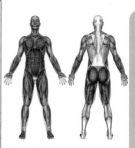

Modification

Easier: Bend the arm supporting your torso, keeping the elbow aligned below your shoulder. Press into your forearm to lift your body into position.

1

2

Level
· Beginner

Duration
· 1½–2 minutes

Benefits
· Stabilizes the spine
· Strenghtens core

Caution
· Lower-back pain
· Wrist issues
· Shoulder pain

Annotation Key
* indicates deep muscles

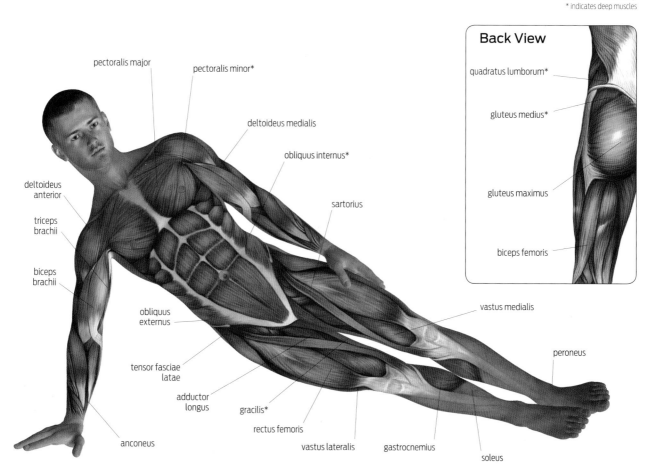

pectoralis major

pectoralis minor*

deltoideus medialis

obliquus internus*

sartorius

deltoideus anterior

triceps brachii

biceps brachii

obliquus externus

tensor fasciae latae

adductor longus

gracilis*

rectus femoris

vastus lateralis

gastrocnemius

soleus

vastus medialis

peroneus

anconeus

Back View

quadratus lumborum*

gluteus medius*

gluteus maximus

biceps femoris

Alternating Crunch

The Alternating Crunch is an advanced version of the Crunch (see pages 56–57). It targets the obliques, in addition to the rectus abdominis. As with the Alternating Sit-Up (see pages 68–69), it is an exercise upon which the foundations of abdominal and core strength are built.

1 Begin by lying down on your back with your legs bent and your palms placed behind your head, elbows flared outward.

2 Raise your head and shoulders off the ground while contracting your trunk toward your waist.

Correct form
· Maintain a precise and short range of motion.
· Keep the back straight and abs taut.

Avoid
· Using the neck to rise.
· Bouncy and speedy repetitions.
· Twisting the shoulders or back as you raise your torso.

Modification

Harder: Place one foot on top of the other thigh near the knee. As you rise, reach your opposite elbow toward the knee of your raised leg. Do 6 repetitions on each side.

3 From this half-sitting position, rotate your torso to bring your left elbow toward your right knee.

4 Lower your head and shoulders back to the floor then raise them again, this time bringing your right elbow toward your left knee. Repeat, doing 20 repetitions per side.

Level
· Beginner

Duration
· 2–3 minutes

Benefits
· Strengthens core
· Works obliques

Caution ⚠
· Lower-back pain
· Shoulder issues

Annotation Key
* indicates deep muscles

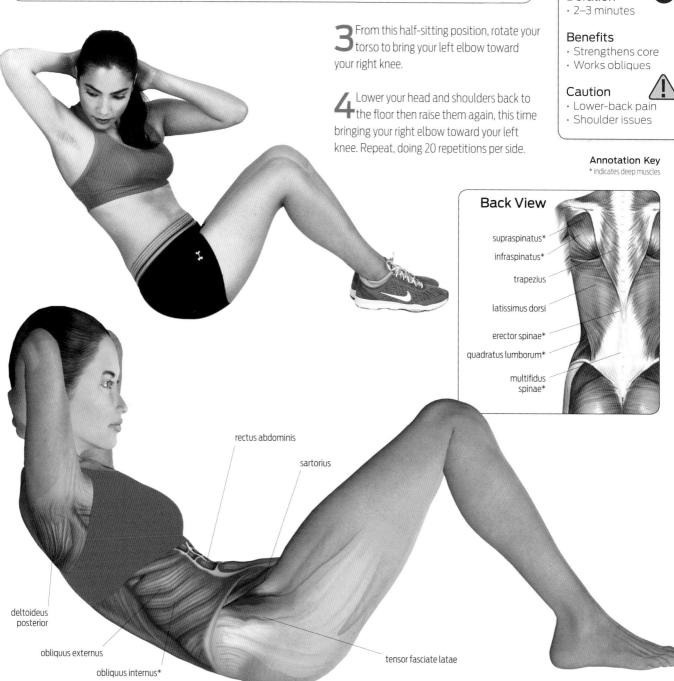

Back View

supraspinatus*
infraspinatus*
trapezius
latissimus dorsi
erector spinae*
quadratus lumborum*
multifidus spinae*

rectus abdominis
sartorius

deltoideus posterior

obliquus externus

obliquus internus*

tensor fasciate latae

Tiny Steps

This simple and easy-to-do exercise targets your abs and can be used to strengthen the lower back. The key to the exercise is good form and slow, deliberate movements.

1 Begin by lying on your back with your knees bent. Place your hands on your hip bones.

2 Raise your right leg, bringing the knee toward your chest while drawing your abdominals into your spine. Hold for up to 10 seconds.

3 Slowly lower your leg to the floor, keeping your abdominals tightened. Switch legs. Repeat 6 times each side.

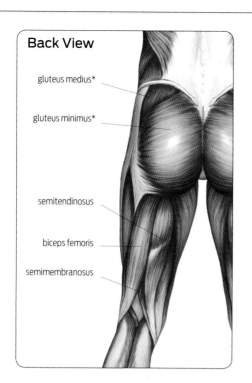

Back View

- gluteus medius*
- gluteus minimus*
- semitendinosus
- biceps femoris
- semimembranosus

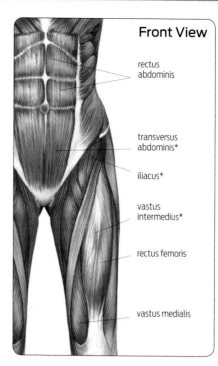

Front View

- rectus abdominis
- transversus abdominis*
- iliacus*
- vastus intermedius*
- rectus femoris
- vastus medialis

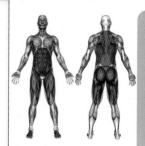

Level
· Beginner

Duration
· 2–3 minutes

Benefits
· Increases lower-abdominal stability
· Helps protect the lower back

Caution
· Lower-back pain

Annotation Key
* indicates deep muscles

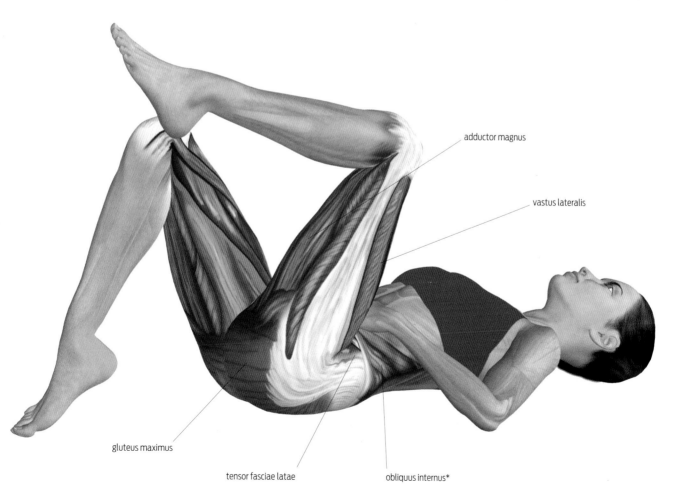

adductor magnus

vastus lateralis

gluteus maximus

tensor fasciae latae

obliquus internus*

Chair Pose

This is a standing yoga posture that tones the entire body, particularly the upper thighs. Because of the length of the hold, it can be a challenging exercise for your thighs and it gets your heart pumping quickly, building stamina and strengthening the core.

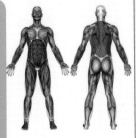

Level
· Beginner

Duration
· 1–2 minutes

Benefits
· Strengthens thighs and hamstrings
· Works core muscles

Caution
· Lower-back pain

Correct form
· Keep your abdominals contracted.
· Maintain good posture.

Avoid
· Arching your back as you lower your body.

1 Start by standing in an upright position, shoulders back and relaxed.

2 Raise your arms over your head, bend your knees, and extend your upper body forward to a 45-degree angle.

3 Keep your feet flat, and push through your heels. Hold for 30–60 seconds.

triceps brachii

deltoideus medialis

rectus abdominis

rectus femoris

vastus lateralis

Side-Lift Bend

The Side-Lift Bend is a challenging move for core and shoulder-girdle endurance. It particularly targets your obliques and quadratus lumborum. The exercise can also be performed with your lower arm outstretched in line with your torso.

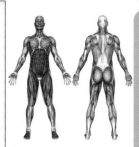

Level
· Advanced

Duration
· 2–3 minutes

Benefits
· Aids core stability
· Strengthens quads

Caution
· Wrist pain
· Shoulder issues

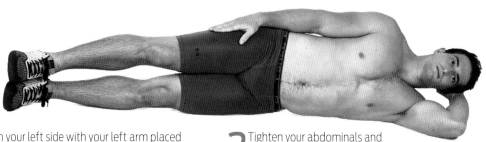

1 Lie on your left side with your left arm placed behind your head and your right arm lying flat on top of your thigh. Tightly press your legs together.

2 Tighten your abdominals and lift both legs off the floor.

Annotation Key
*indicates deep muscles

3 Sliding your right hand down your outstretched leg, lift your head and crunch your oblique muscles from your upper body and lower body simultaneously. Repeat 10 times on each side.

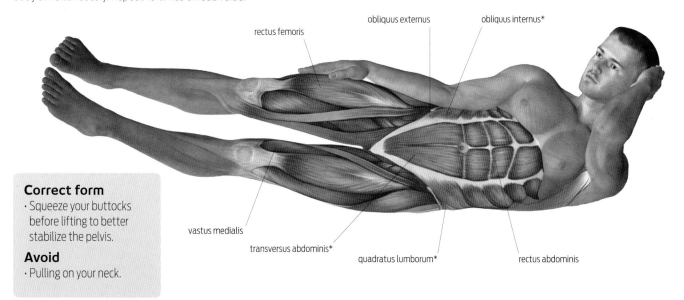

rectus femoris

obliquus externus

obliquus internus*

vastus medialis

transversus abdominis*

quadratus lumborum*

rectus abdominis

Correct form
· Squeeze your buttocks before lifting to better stabilize the pelvis.

Avoid
· Pulling on your neck.

Quadruped

An excellent stability exercise that calls for many muscles to work together in order to perform the movement, the Quadruped is particularly effective for developing the core and lower back. Extension of the shoulders and hips means that it gives both upper and lower body parts a great workout, too, while improving coordination and balance.

Correct form
· Maintain a flat back throughout the exercise.

Avoid
· Using any jerky movements.

1 Begin on all fours with your hands, knees, and feet shoulder-width apart.

2 Fully extend one leg while straightening the opposite arm in front. Hold the position for 10 seconds, contracting your abs and tensing your thigh muscles. Keep as still as possible.

3 Lower the leg and arm slowly, returning to the start position.

4 Perform 2 repetitions and then repeat the whole exercise using the other leg and arm.

Modification

Harder: Instead of kneeling, press into a plank position to begin, and then raise the opposite arm and leg.

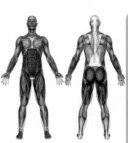

Level
· Beginner

Duration
· 1½–2 minutes

Benefits
· Tones arms, legs, and abdominals

Caution
· Knee issues
· Lower-back pain

Annotation Key
* indicates deep muscles

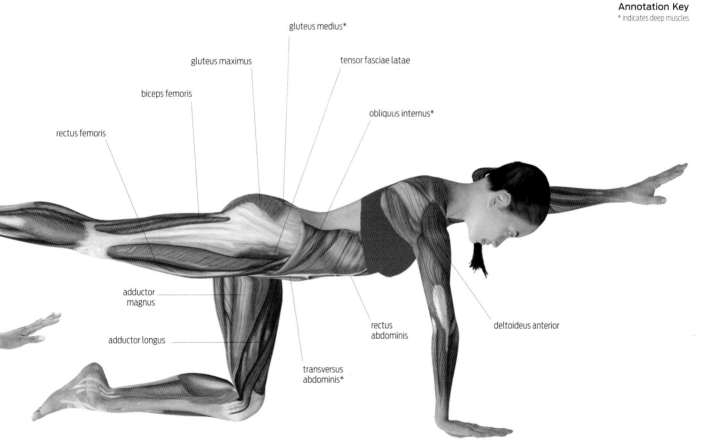

gluteus medius*

gluteus maximus

tensor fasciae latae

biceps femoris

obliquus internus*

rectus femoris

adductor magnus

adductor longus

rectus abdominis

deltoideus anterior

transversus abdominis*

Clamshell Series

The Clamshell Series is a simple and effective exercise for abdominal stabilization, and for working the abductors and adductors; it also increases pelvic stability. If your technique is good, your glutes and hamstrings will be strengthened, since this exercise activates both the gluteus medius and gluteus maximus. Use a resistance band around your knees, if you want more of a challenge.

Correct form
· Perform each movement slowly and under control.

Avoid
· Allowing your hips to twist or rise while lifting your knees.

1 Lie on your right hip, placing your right forearm on the floor for support. Put your left hand on your left hip. Have your legs slightly bent, one on top of the other.

2 Keeping a straight spine, your right leg on the floor, and your feet together and on the floor, lift your left knee 10 times.

3 After the last repetition, with your knees and feet together, lift both of your feet off the floor.

4 While your feet are raised, again open and close your knees 10 times, moving only your left leg.

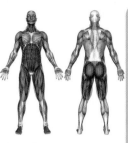

Back View

quadratus lumborum*

gluteus medius*

gluteus maximus

biceps femoris

adductor magnus

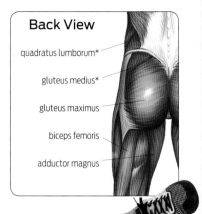

5 Finish step 4 with your knees open, then straighten your left leg, without moving the thigh. Bend the leg again. Do this 10 times. Switch sides and repeat the entire series.

Level
· Intermediate

Duration
· 3–4 minutes

Benefits
· Increases pelvic stability
· Strengthens adductor muscles

Caution
· Knee pain
· Hamstring stiffness
· Lower-back pain

Annotation Key
* indicates deep muscles

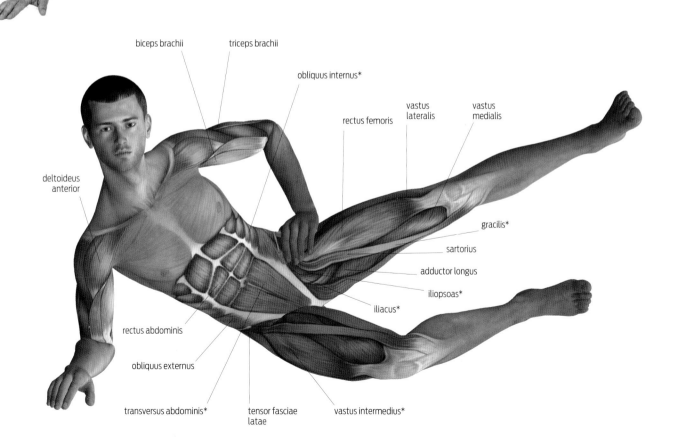

biceps brachii

triceps brachii

obliquus internus*

rectus femoris

vastus lateralis

vastus medialis

deltoideus anterior

gracilis*

sartorius

adductor longus

iliopsoas*

iliacus*

rectus abdominis

obliquus externus

transversus abdominis*

tensor fasciae latae

vastus intermedius*

Kneeling Side Lift

Tone the outer thigh and core with this Pilates exercise. Take care not to let the extended foot touch the floor until the movement is complete. The exercise can be made easier by propping up your torso on one arm.

Correct form
· Keep your torso aligned to balance the movement of your leg.

Avoid
· Sinking your neck into your shoulders.

1 Begin by kneeling on the floor, with your left leg outstretched to the side and the right leg up under the hips. Place both hands behind your head, with your elbows extended out to the sides.

2 Lift your left leg up off the floor, bringing it as high as your hips. Repeat the whole sequence 5–6 times.

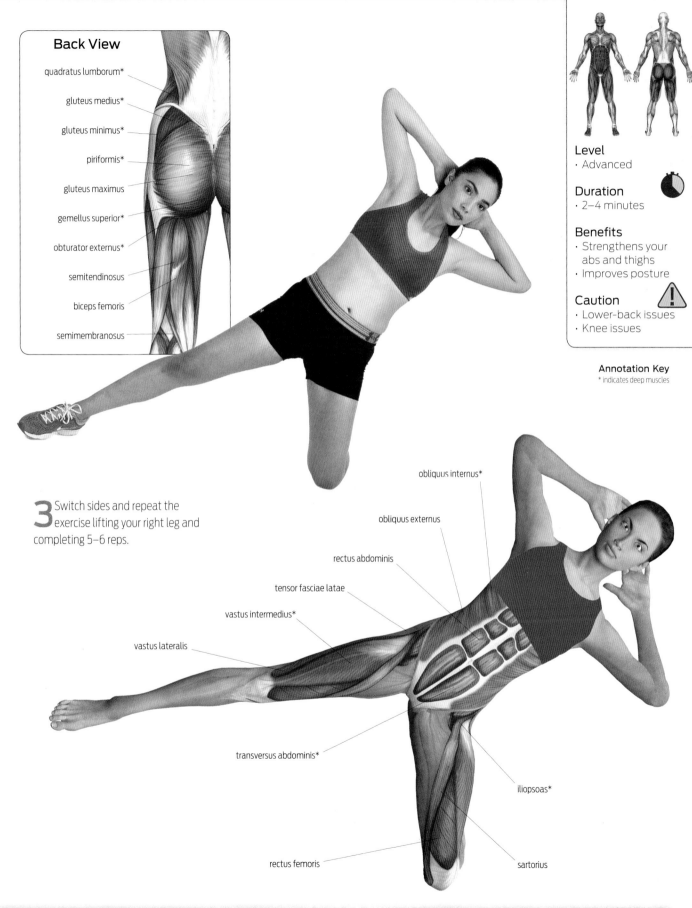

Back View

quadratus lumborum*

gluteus medius*

gluteus minimus*

piriformis*

gluteus maximus

gemellus superior*

obturator externus*

semitendinosus

biceps femoris

semimembranosus

Level
· Advanced

Duration
· 2–4 minutes

Benefits
· Strengthens your abs and thighs
· Improves posture

Caution
· Lower-back issues
· Knee issues

Annotation Key
indicates deep muscles

3 Switch sides and repeat the exercise lifting your right leg and completing 5–6 reps.

obliquus internus*

obliquus externus

rectus abdominis

tensor fasciae latae

vastus intermedius*

vastus lateralis

transversus abdominis*

iliopsoas*

rectus femoris

sartorius

Forward Lunge

The Forward Lunge takes you into a huge lunge, working the muscles of your lower body as well as the lower portion of your abdomen. It helps stretch and strengthen the thighs, particularly the hip flexors, and it opens up the groin region, tones the calves, and strengthens the lower back.

Correct form
· Lengthen your spine by maintaining the correct position in your shoulders and upper body.

Avoid
· Dropping your extended leg so the knee touches the floor.

1 Standing tall, move your right foot forward and bend at the hips, bringing your hands down to either side of your foot.

2 Step back with the left foot, keeping your legs in line with your hips, and place your hands on the floor, elbows locked. Keep the ball of your right foot in contact with the floor.

3 Press the ball of your right foot on the floor, contract your thigh muscles, and press up to maintain your left leg in a straight position. Hold for 5–6 seconds.

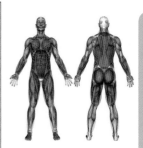

Level
· Beginner

Duration
· 1–3 minutes

Benefits
· Stretches and strengthens thighs
· Mobilizes groin

Caution
· Lower-back pain
· Wrist pain
· Shoulder problems

Back View

levator scapulae*

splenius*

trapezius

4 Slowly return to standing position, and then repeat on the other side. Do up to 10 reps on each side.

Annotation Key
* indicates deep muscles

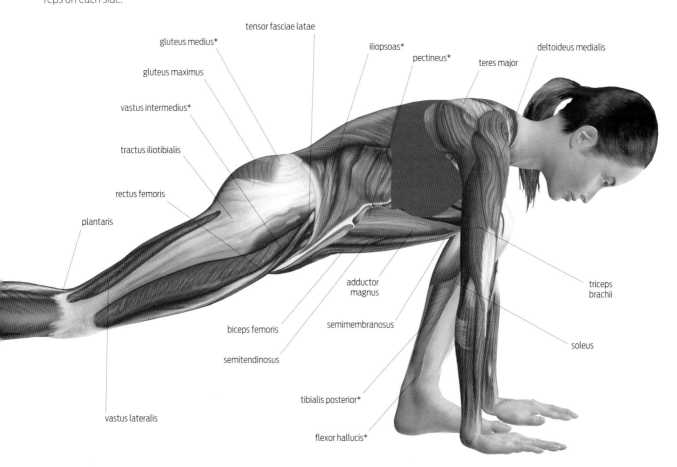

tensor fasciae latae

gluteus medius*

iliopsoas*

pectineus*

teres major

deltoideus medialis

gluteus maximus

vastus intermedius*

tractus iliotibialis

rectus femoris

plantaris

triceps brachii

adductor magnus

soleus

biceps femoris

semimembranosus

semitendinosus

tibialis posterior*

vastus lateralis

flexor hallucis*

Reverse Lunge with Lateral Extension

Although a more complex movement, compared to the basic Lunge, this exercise places less stress on the knees while still toning the entire length of your legs and the torso.

Correct form
· Keep your shoulders pressed downward.
· Keep your neck relaxed.
· Make sure your upper body is upright as you lower and then raise your leg.

Avoid
· Twisting either hip.
· Hunching your shoulders.
· Arching your back or hunching forward.

1 From a standing position, step your right leg back, resting the toes on the floor.

2 Bend both knees as you move into a lunge position. Lower your body, flexing your left knee and hip until your right lower leg is almost in contact with the floor.

3 Raise your arms to the side until they are level with your shoulders.

4 Return to starting position by extending the hip and knee of your left leg and bringing your right leg forward to meet your left. Repeat with the opposite leg. Complete 10 lunges on each side.

Back View

erector spinae*

gluteus medius*

gluteus minimus*

obturator externus

semitendinosus

semimembranosus

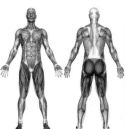

Level
· Beginner

Duration
· 2–4 minutes

Benefits
· Strengthens gluteal and leg muscles
· Improves posture

Caution
· Arm or shoulder injury
· Knee issues

Annotation Key
* indicates deep muscles

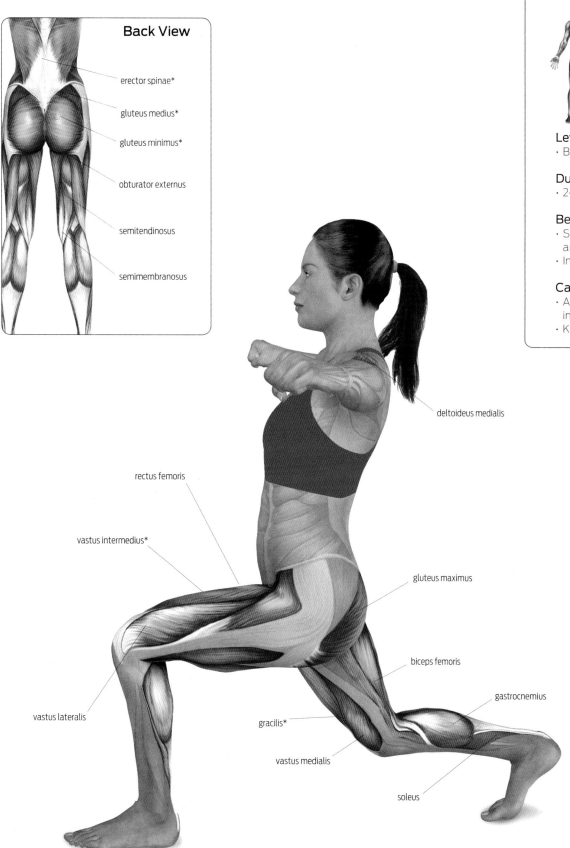

deltoideus medialis

rectus femoris

vastus intermedius*

gluteus maximus

biceps femoris

gastrocnemius

vastus lateralis

gracilis*

vastus medialis

soleus

Seated Russian Twist

This is an exercise that works the muscles of the abdomen by performing a twisting motion at your midriff. The Russian Twist is used to build explosiveness in the upper torso, which can help in sports such as baseball and golf.

1 Sit with your knees bent and your feet flat on the floor. Lift up through your torso. Raise your arms extended in front, so that your hands are outstretched above your knees.

2 Rotate your upper body to the right, keeping your arms parallel with the floor.

3 Pass through the center and rotate to the left. Repeat ten times on each side.

Modification

Harder: Lift your feet off the floor, and rotate your torso from side to side, pulling your knees in and out as you twist.

1

2

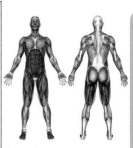

Level
· Intermediate

Duration
· ½–1 minute

Benefits
· Increases abdominal endurance

Caution
· Shoulder pain
· Lower-back issues

Annotation Key
* indicates deep muscles

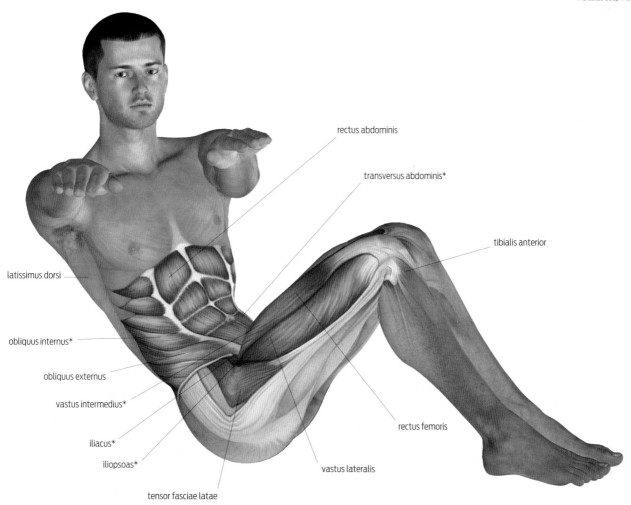

rectus abdominis

transversus abdominis*

tibialis anterior

latissimus dorsi

obliquus internus*

obliquus externus

vastus intermedius*

iliacus*

iliopsoas*

rectus femoris

vastus lateralis

tensor fasciae latae

Chair Squat

Chair Squats can be performed anywhere: In your kitchen, at your office desk, or in your hotel room. They are particularly beneficial for beginner exercisers, those learning proper squatting technique, and those with conditions that affect balance or coordination.

1 Stand upright in front of the chair. Clasp your hands, and position them in front of your chest

2 Slowly lower your body into a squat position.

3 Continue lowering until you are resting on the chair.

4 With control, rise back up to the starting position, and repeat, aiming for 10 repetitions.

Correct form
· Gaze forward and keep your back straight.

Avoid
· Arching your back or hunching forward.

Front View

rectus abdominis

transversus
abdominis*

Back View

erector spinae*

gluteus maximus

obturator externus

adductor magnus

semitendinosus

semimembranosus

gastrocnemius

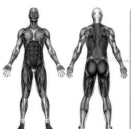

Level
· Beginner

Duration
· ½–1 minute

Benefits
· Restores mobility
  after injury
· Counteracts
  sedentary lifestyle

Caution
· Hip issues
· Knee issues
· Lower-back pain

Annotation Key
* indicates deep muscles

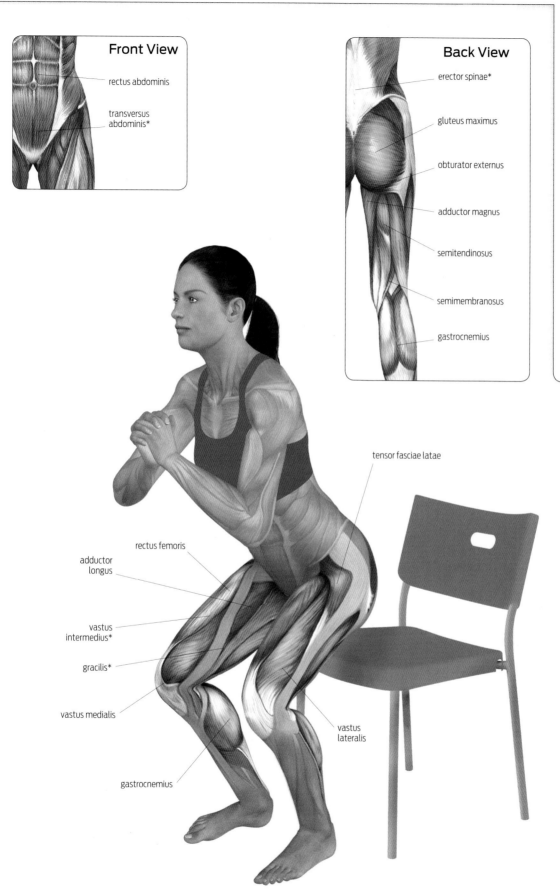

tensor fasciae latae

rectus femoris

adductor
longus

vastus
intermedius*

gracilis*

vastus medialis

gastrocnemius

vastus
lateralis

Chair Dip

The Chair Dip is a great body-weight exercise that builds arm and shoulder strength, particularly the triceps. Like the Chair Squat (pages 98–99), this simple exercise can be done almost anywhere with just a sturdy chair.

Correct form
· Keep your body close to the chair.
· Keep your spine in neutral position throughout the movement.

Avoid
· Allowing your shoulders to lift toward your ears.

1 Sit up tall near the front of a sturdy chair. Place your hands beside your hips, wrapping your fingers over the front edge of the chair.

2 Extend your legs in front of you, and place your feet flat on the floor.

3 Scoot off the edge of the chair until your knees align directly above your feet and your torso will be able to clear the chair as you dip down.

4 Bending your elbows directly behind you, without splaying them out to the sides, lower your torso until your elbows make a 90-degree angle.

5 Press into the chair, raising your body back to the starting position. Repeat up to 15 times.

Modification

Harder: Keeping your knees squeezed together, perform the dips with one leg lifted straight out, parallel to the floor. Repeat 15 times on each side.

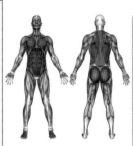

Level
· Beginner

Duration
· 2–3 minutes

Benefits
· Strengthens the shoulder girdle

Caution
· Back issues
· Shoulder or wrist injury

Annotation Key
* indicates deep muscles

Front View

pectoralis major

pectoralis minor*

coracobrachialis*

deltoideus anterior

biceps brachii

deltoideus posterior

triceps brachii

rectus abdominis

obliquus externus

transversus abdominis*

latissimus dorsi

gluteus maximus

Push-Up

A basic Push-Up is one of the most effective ways to strengthen your chest and arm muscles. There are literally dozens of variations on this exercise, but simple push-ups require no equipment other than your own body weight, and they can be done anywhere there is a flat surface with enough space for you to stretch out.

1 Begin facedown, with your hands planted on the floor, shoulder-width apart, and your arms fully extended. Lengthen your legs, and balance on your toes.

2 Bend your arms until your chest is nearly touching the floor, then push back to full extension. Complete 3 sets of 10 repetitions.

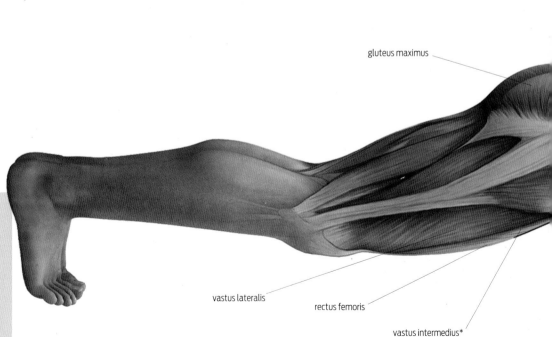

gluteus maximus

vastus lateralis

rectus femoris

vastus intermedius*

Correct form
· Keep your chest directly over your hands.
· Use your arms and legs, not your back.

Avoid
· Arching or dipping your back.

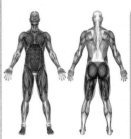

Modification

Easier: This exercise can be made easier by bracing your knees on the ground.

Level
· Intermediate

Duration
· 2–3 minutes

Benefits
· Helps strengthen and stabilize the upper body

Caution
· Leg issues
· Ankle problems
· Lower-back pain

Annotation Key
* indicates deep muscles

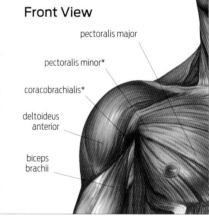

Front View

pectoralis major

pectoralis minor*

coracobrachialis*

deltoideus anterior

biceps brachii

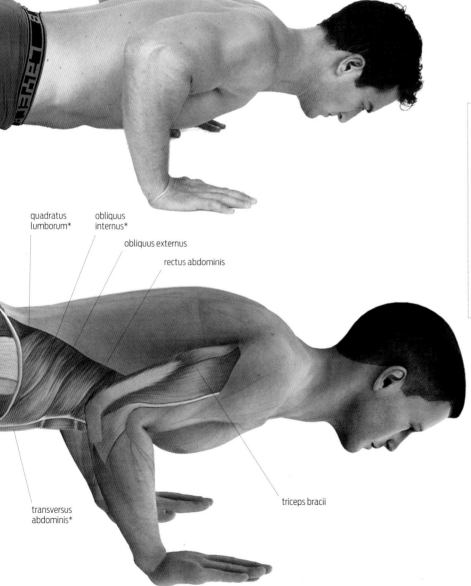

quadratus lumborum*

obliquus internus*

obliquus externus

rectus abdominis

transversus abdominis*

triceps bracii

Prone Trunk Raise

This is a relatively simple exercise that not only strengthens the triceps and shoulders, but also stretches the back and chest, whilst tightening the muscles in your abs and adductors.

1 Lie prone on the floor. Bend your elbows, placing your hands flat on the floor on either side of your chest. Keep your elbows pulled in toward your body. Separate your legs hip-width apart, and extend through your toes. The tops of your feet should be touching the floor.

2 Inhale, and press against the floor with your hands and the tops of your feet, lifting your torso and hips off the floor. Contract your thighs, and tuck your tailbone toward your pubis.

3 Lift through the top of your chest, fully extending your arms and creating an arch in your back from your upper torso. Push your shoulders down and back, and elongate your neck as you gaze slightly upward.

4 Hold for 15–30 seconds, and exhale as you lower yourself to the floor.

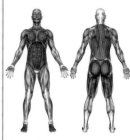

Front View

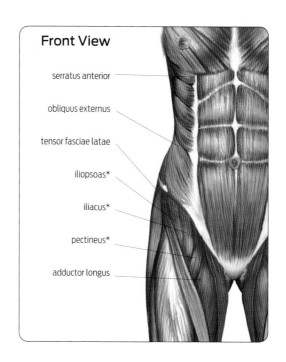

- serratus anterior
- obliquus externus
- tensor fasciae latae
- iliopsoas*
- iliacus*
- pectineus*
- adductor longus

Level
· Intermediate

Duration
· 1–2 minutes

Benefits
· Increases upper body strength

Caution
· Shoulder issues
· Hip issues
· Lower-back pain

Annotation Key
* indicates deep muscles

Modification

Easier: This exercise can be modified by bending the legs to reduce stress on the abdominals.

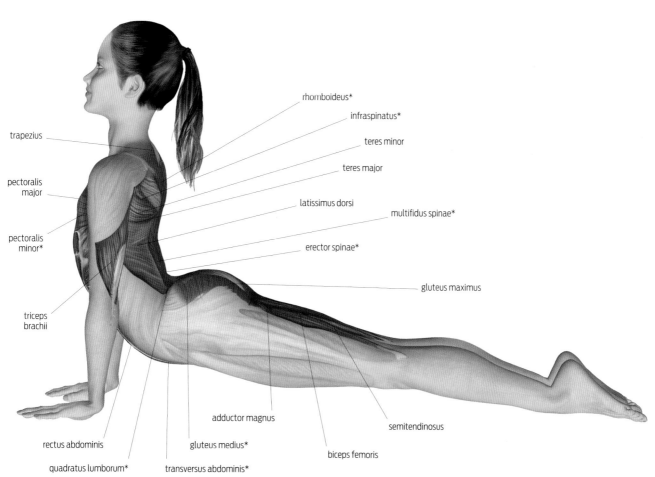

- trapezius
- pectoralis major
- pectoralis minor*
- triceps brachii
- rectus abdominis
- quadratus lumborum*
- gluteus medius*
- transversus abdominis*
- adductor magnus
- biceps femoris
- rhomboideus*
- infraspinatus*
- teres minor
- teres major
- latissimus dorsi
- multifidus spinae*
- erector spinae*
- gluteus maximus
- semitendinosus

Spine Twist

Stretching and strengthening the back, the Spine Twist is an excellent exercise for increasing the range of motion in the torso and spine, which helps to prevent injury.

Correct form
· Keep your hips facing forward throughout the exercise.

Avoid
· Raising your hips off the floor.

1 Sit on the ground with your legs extended and your feet together. Hold your back straight, and raise your arms out to the sides, fully extended, at 90 degrees to your torso.

2 Keeping your abdominals pulled in, twist your waist to the right, taking your entire upper body with it, then return to the central position.

3 Repeat the movement, this time turning to the left. Return to the center.

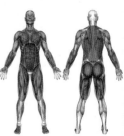

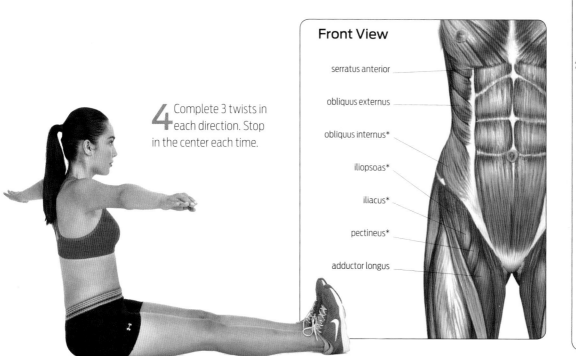

Front View

- serratus anterior
- obliquus externus
- obliquus internus*
- iliopsoas*
- iliacus*
- pectineus*
- adductor longus

4 Complete 3 twists in each direction. Stop in the center each time.

Level
- Intermediate

Duration
- 1–2 minutes

Benefits
- Improves back flexibility
- Strengthens and lengthens the torso

Caution
- Lower-back pain
- Hip issues

Annotation Key
*indicates deep muscles

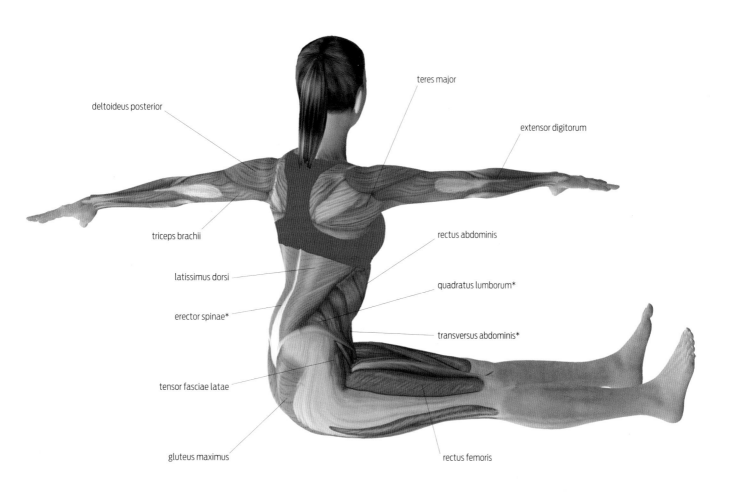

- deltoideus posterior
- teres major
- extensor digitorum
- triceps brachii
- rectus abdominis
- latissimus dorsi
- quadratus lumborum*
- erector spinae*
- transversus abdominis*
- tensor fasciae latae
- gluteus maximus
- rectus femoris

Bicycle Crunch

Whilst relatively easy to perform, the Bicycle Crunch is widely regarded as one of the most effective exercises you can do to achieve perfect abs and obliques. Good form is important since this is the best way to achieve results.

1 Lie supine on the floor with your knees bent. Bring your hands behind your head. Lift your legs off the floor.

2 Roll up with your torso, reaching your right elbow to your left knee while extending the right leg in front of you. Imagine pulling your shoulder blades off the floor and twisting from your ribs and oblique muscles.

3 Switch sides. Move through the movement as you would cycle on a bike. Cycle 6 times on each side.

Correct form
· Keep your chin off your chest.
· Keep both hips on the floor

Avoid
· Pulling with your hands.
· Arching your back.

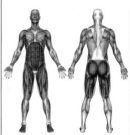

1

2

Modification

Easier: Begin with both feet on the floor. Place your left ankle on your right thigh, near the knee. Reach your right elbow toward your left knee. Complete 6 repetitions on each side.

Level
· Intermediate

Duration
· 2 minutes

Benefits
· Stabilizes the core and strengthens the abdominals

Caution
· Hip or knee issues
· Lower-back pain
· Neck problems

Annotation Key
* indicates deep muscles

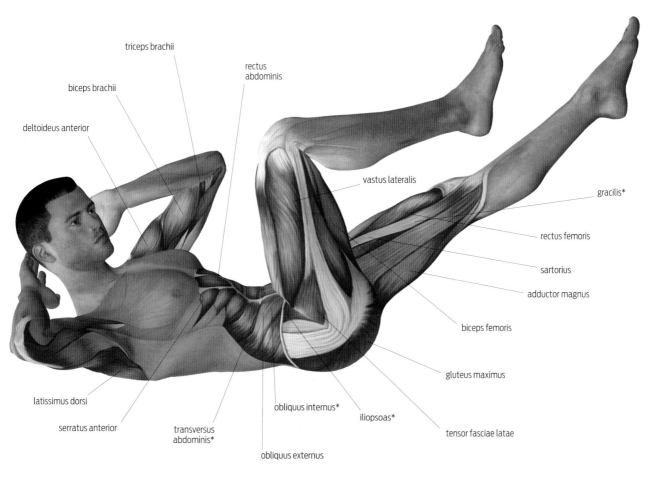

triceps brachii

biceps brachii

deltoideus anterior

rectus abdominis

vastus lateralis

gracilis*

rectus femoris

sartorius

adductor magnus

biceps femoris

gluteus maximus

latissimus dorsi

serratus anterior

transversus abdominis*

obliquus internus*

iliopsoas*

obliquus externus

tensor fasciae latae

Plank

The Plank is one of the best exercises you can do for your core because it builds isometric strength to help sculpt your waistline and improve your posture. It's not about balance, so much as it is about crafting a solid, bodily structure with which you can distribute force production in relation to the ground.

Correct form
- Keep your abdominal muscles tight and your body in a straight line.

Avoid
- Bridging too high, since this can take stress off the working muscles.

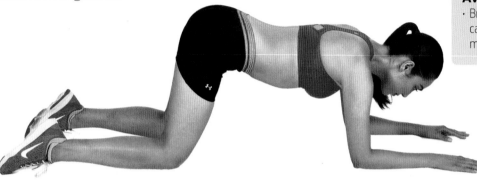

1 Position yourself on all fours, then plant your forearms on the floor parallel to one another, with 90-degree bends at the elbows

2 Raise your knees off the ground, and lengthen your legs until they are straight and in line with your body. Keep your weight shifted over your feet. Hold for 30 seconds (building up to 120 seconds).

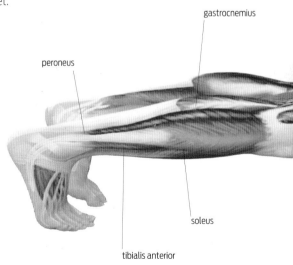

gastrocnemius

peroneus

soleus

tibialis anterior

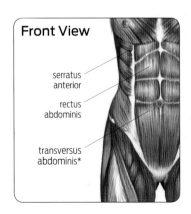

Front View

serratus anterior

rectus abdominis

transversus abdominis*

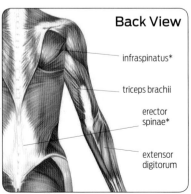

Back View

infraspinatus*

triceps brachii

erector spinae*

extensor digitorum

Modification

Harder: Instead of resting on your forearms, extend your arms fully when on all fours, then continue with step 2.

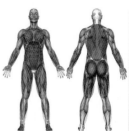

Level
· Beginner

Duration
· 1–2 minutes

Benefits
· Increases overall body strength

Caution
· Knee or hip issues
· Lower-back pain

Annotation Key
* indicates deep muscles

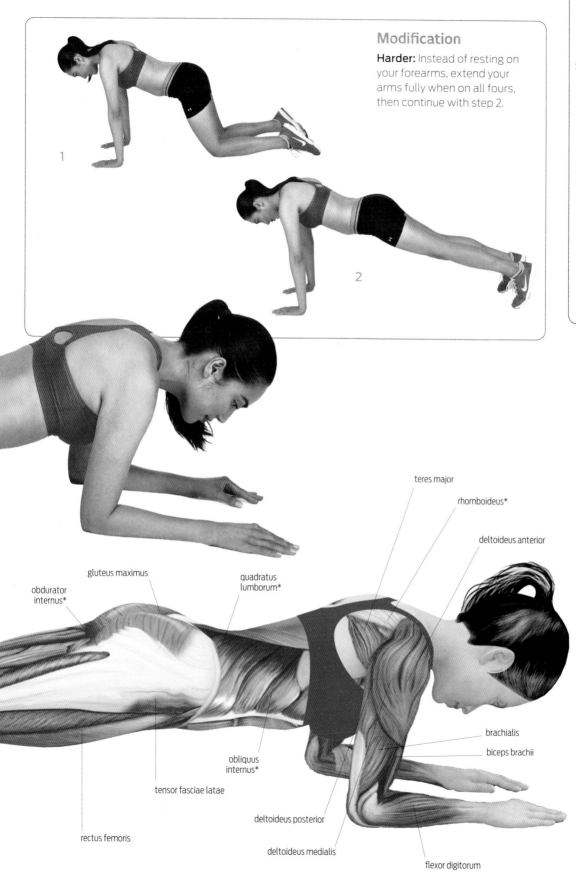

teres major

rhomboideus*

deltoideus anterior

gluteus maximus

obdurator internus*

quadratus lumborum*

brachialis

biceps brachii

obliquus internus*

tensor fasciae latae

deltoideus posterior

rectus femoris

deltoideus medialis

flexor digitorum

Chair Plié

The Chair Plié is a squat exercise that primarily targets the outer thighs and, to a lesser degree, the groin, quads, glutes, hamstrings, and hip flexors. Find a sturdy chair and do it anywhere!

1 Stand with your feet in a wide stance, with toes turned out and the chair in front of you.

2 Keeping your knees aligned with your toes, bend your knees and lower your body into a squat position.

3 Keeping your back straight, raise yourself back to starting position. Perform 10 repetitions.

Correct form
· Keep your upper body braced.
· Remain in control when squatting.
· A precise range of motion.

Avoid
· Lowering butt past knees.
· Stressing your lower back.
· Swinging with momentum.

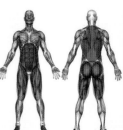

Back View

erector spinae*

gluteus maximus

vastus lateralis

adductor magnus

semitendinosus

biceps femoris

semimembranosus

Level
· Beginner

Duration
· ½–1 minute

Benefits
· Engages and tones
  thigh muscles

Caution
· Ankle problems
· Knee issues
· Back or hip pain

Annotation Key
* indicates deep muscles

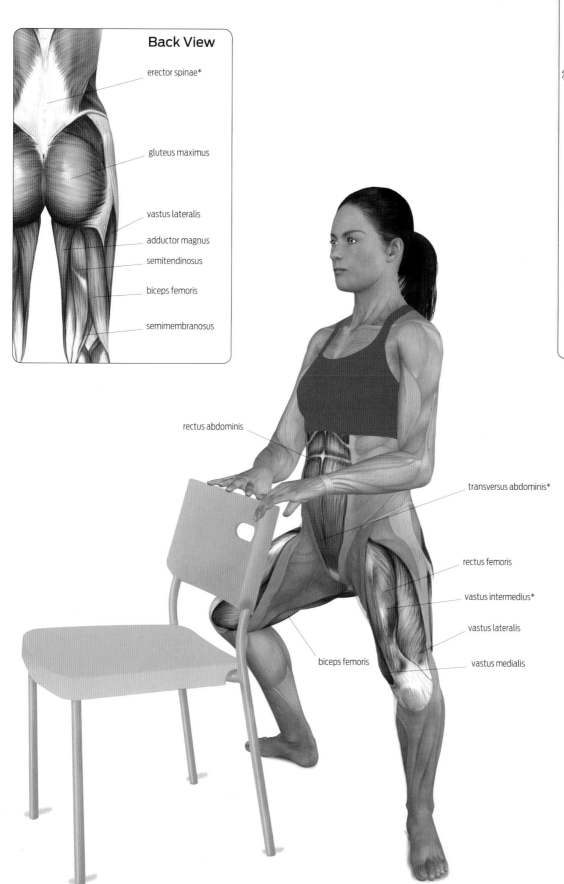

rectus abdominis

transversus abdominis*

rectus femoris

vastus intermedius*

vastus lateralis

biceps femoris

vastus medialis

Lateral Low Lunge

The Lateral Low Lunge enhances the mobility of your hips, and helps loosen the muscles of your glutes and groin. It requires balance, strength, and coordination. Be sure to have properly stretched your thigh muscles before attempting this exercise.

Level
· Beginner

Duration
· 1½–2 minutes

Benefits
· Engages and tones inner-thigh adductors

Caution
· Shoulder issues
· Arm issues
· Back pain

Annotation Key
* indicates deep muscles

1 Stand upright with your arms outstretched in front of you, parallel to the floor.

2 Step out to the right. Squat down on your right leg and bend at the hips. Keeping your feet flat on the floor, extend your left leg.

3 Squeeze your buttocks and press off your right leg to return to the standing position. Perform 10 repetitions on each side.

transversus abdominis

adductor longus

vastus lateralis

adductor magnus

sartorius

rectus femoris

Correct form
· Your spine remains neutral as you bend your hips.

Avoid
· Craning your neck as you perform the movement.

Hand-to-Toe Lift

The Hand-to-Toe Lift is a challenging exercise that will increase abdominal and leg stability. It can be made more difficult by adding this step before lowering your leg: swing your left leg out to the side, still holding your toes. Breathe steadily, and hold for about 5 seconds.

Level
· Intermediate

Duration
· 2–3 minutes

Benefits
· Engages and tones inner-thigh adductors

Caution
· Back pain
· Shoulder issues

Annotation Key
* indicates deep muscles

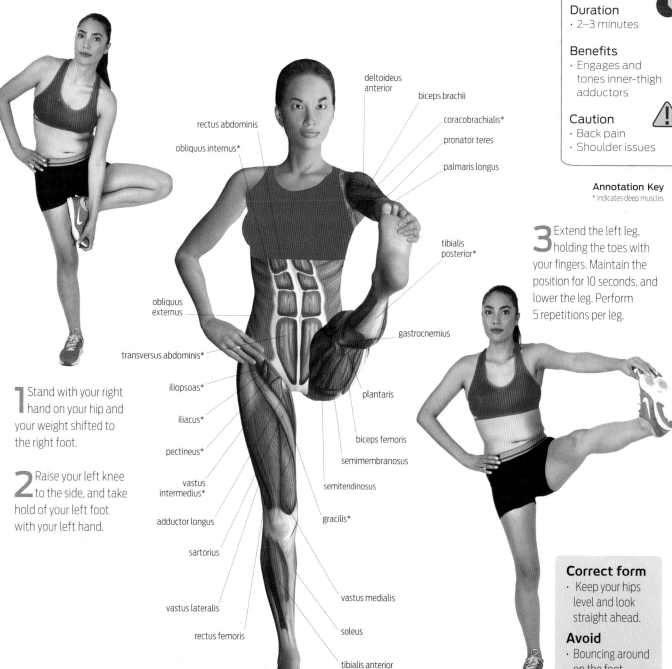

deltoideus anterior

biceps brachii

coracobrachialis*

pronator teres

palmaris longus

rectus abdominis

obliquus internus*

tibialis posterior*

obliquus externus

gastrocnemius

transversus abdominis*

plantaris

iliopsoas*

iliacus*

biceps femoris

pectineus*

semimembranosus

vastus intermedius*

semitendinosus

adductor longus

gracilis*

sartorius

vastus medialis

vastus lateralis

soleus

rectus femoris

tibialis anterior

1 Stand with your right hand on your hip and your weight shifted to the right foot.

2 Raise your left knee to the side, and take hold of your left foot with your left hand.

3 Extend the left leg, holding the toes with your fingers. Maintain the position for 10 seconds, and lower the leg. Perform 5 repetitions per leg.

Correct form
· Keep your hips level and look straight ahead.

Avoid
· Bouncing around on the foot.

Single-Leg Balance

You can improve your muscle strength by performing even the most simple exercises. The single-leg stance is also very effective for improving balance. It is easy to do as part of your home-exercise program, or during your lunch break, and it can be modified to increase the challenge as your confidence and strength improve.

Correct form
· Maintain an erect posture throughout the exercise.

Avoid
· Removing your hands from your hips.

1 Stand with your hands on your hips, and raise your right leg, bent at the knee, directly in front of you at a 90-degree angle. Hold for 15 seconds.

2 Press your right leg down and forward, though not touching the floor, and hold for 15 seconds.

3 Finally, press your right leg out to the side, again without touching the floor, and hold for 15 seconds. Complete the entire sequence 3 times, then switch legs.

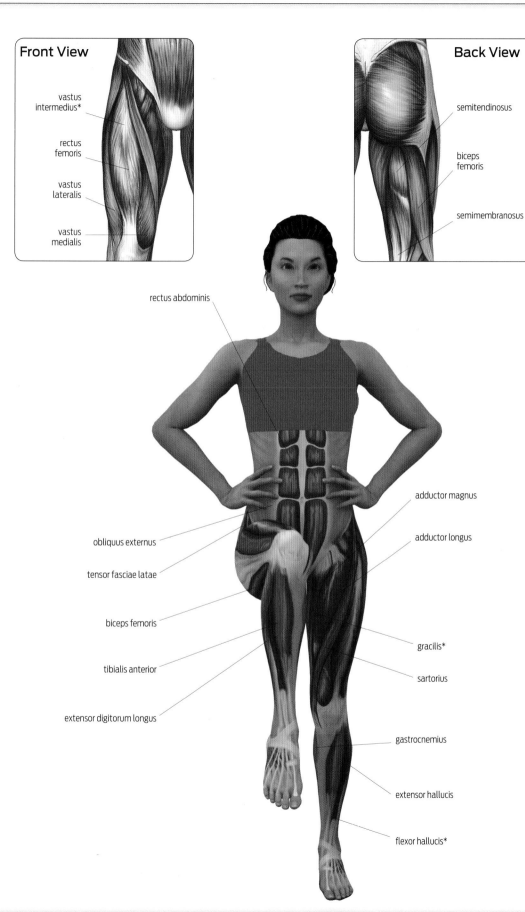

Front View

vastus
intermedius*

rectus
femoris

vastus
lateralis

vastus
medialis

Back View

semitendinosus

biceps
femoris

semimembranosus

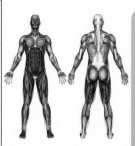

Level
· Intermediate

Duration
· 2–3 minutes

Benefits
· Strengthens the legs
  and core
· Increases core
  stability

Caution
· Lower-back issues
· Knee pain

Annotation Key
* indicates deep muscles

rectus abdominis

obliquus externus

tensor fasciae latae

biceps femoris

tibialis anterior

extensor digitorum longus

adductor magnus

adductor longus

gracilis*

sartorius

gastrocnemius

extensor hallucis

flexor hallucis*

Modification

Harder: This exercise
can be made more
difficult by gently
tapping your heel to
the floor between
steps.

Inverted Hamstring

This is an advanced muscle toning and stretching exercise that primarily targets the hamstrings and to a lesser degree the glutes. The Inverted Hamstring is also excellent for improving balance and core strength and stability.

Correct form
· Your spine is neutral as you progress through the motion.
· Your knees align over your ankles.
· Your body moves slowly.

Avoid
· Allowing your back foot to touch the ground.
· Using your arms to move your body.

1 Begin in a standing position, feet shoulder-width apart, with your knees soft and your arms above your head.

2 Bend forward at the waist while simultaneously spreading your arms out to your sides for balance and lifting your left leg behind you.

3 Continue to bend forward until your torso and leg are roughly parallel to the ground.

4 Return to a standing position, switch legs, and repeat.

Modification
Easier: This exercise can be made easier by holding a balance pole out in front of you.

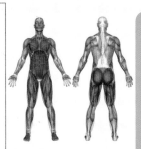

Front View

- deltoideus anterior
- pectoralis major
- pectoralis minor*
- obliquus internus*
- transversus abdominis*
- vastus intermedius*
- sartorius

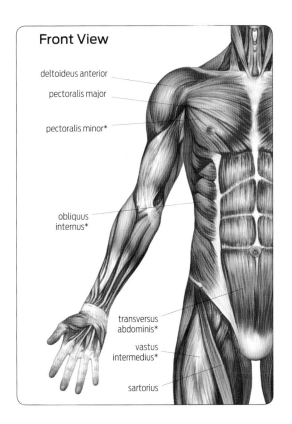

Back View

- gluteus medius*
- gluteus minimus*
- tractus iliotibialis
- gemellus inferior*
- semitendinosus
- plantaris
- semimembranosus

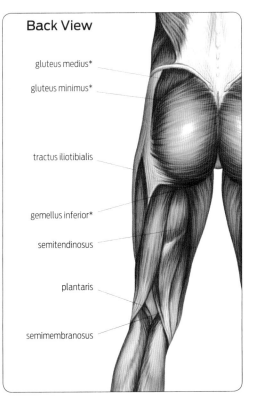

Level
· Advanced

Duration
· 1–2 minutes

Benefits
· Helps stabilize the body
· Strengthens the core

Caution
· Back issues
· Shoulder pain

Annotation Key
* indicates deep muscles

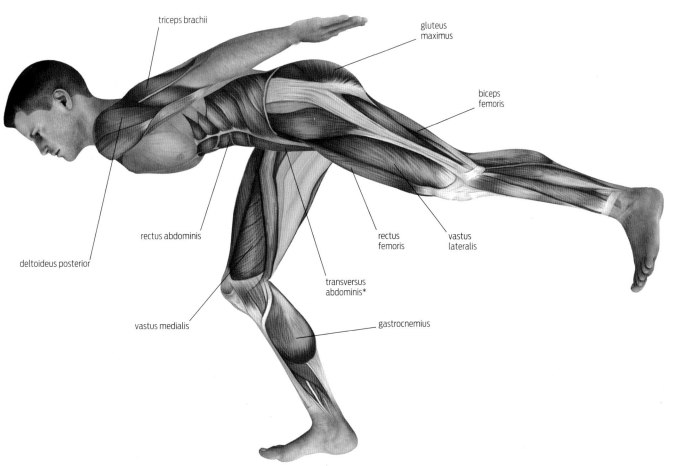

- triceps brachii
- gluteus maximus
- biceps femoris
- rectus abdominis
- deltoideus posterior
- rectus femoris
- vastus lateralis
- transversus abdominis*
- vastus medialis
- gastrocnemius

Side-Lying Hip Abduction

The purpose of this exercise is to strengthen the muscles on the side of your hip. It is a calisthenics and Pilates exercise that primarily targets the glutes and also, to a lesser degree, the obliques, abs, and outer thighs. It gives the upper legs muscle tone.

1 Lie on your left side with your legs extended and your feet stacked one on top of the other. Rest your right arm along your right hip, and use your left arm to support your head.

vastus lateralis

vastus intermedius*

vastus medialis

Correct form
· Keep your body in a straight line.

Avoid
· Raising your leg too high.
· Tipping forward or back.

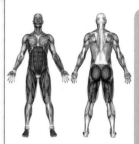

2 Raise your right leg until you feel your core kick in. Hold for 30 seconds, lower, and repeat, then switch sides.

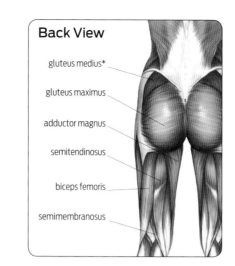

Back View

- gluteus medius*
- gluteus maximus
- adductor magnus
- semitendinosus
- biceps femoris
- semimembranosus

Level
· Beginner

Duration
· 2–3 minutes

Benefits
· Strenghtens glutes and hips
· Tones core

Caution
· Lower-back pain
· Rotator cuff problems

Annotation Key
* indicates deep muscles

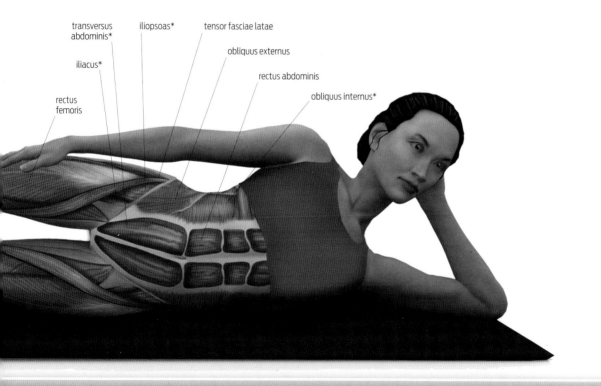

- transversus abdominis*
- iliopsoas*
- tensor fasciae latae
- obliquus externus
- iliacus*
- rectus abdominis
- obliquus internus*
- rectus femoris

Towel Fly

The Towel Fly is a great way to give your chest workout a boost by making the most of your body weight. When you do this exercise, you will also recruit numerous other muscles of the arms, back, hips, and abdomen to stabilize yourself. Master it and you'll see improvement in your core strength.

1 Place a towel on the floor in front of you. Assume the push-up position, with your elbows fully extended, and the towel under your hands.

2 Maintain a rigid plank position and, putting your weight into your heels, move your hands together. The aim is to get the towel to bunch together below your sternum.

3 Straighten out the towel by pressing outward with your arms, returning to the starting position. Repeat 10 times.

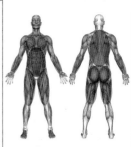

Back View

flexor
carpi radialis

triceps
brachii

teres
minor

brachialis

extensor
carpi radialis

subscapularis*

extensor
digitorum

infraspinatus*

brachioradialis

latissimus dorsi

erector spinae*

quadratus
lumborum*

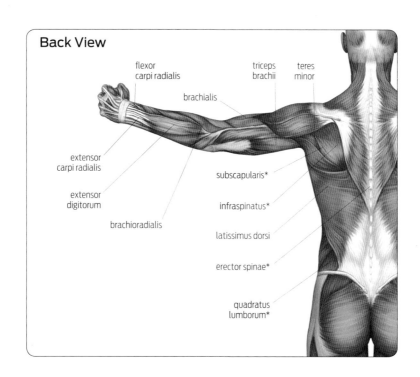

Level
· Advanced

Duration
· 2–3 minutes

Benefits
· Strengthens and
  stabilizes the upper
  body and core

Caution
· Back pain
· Shoulder issues
· Hip problems

Annotation Key
* indicates deep muscles

deltoideus
anterior

deltoideus
posterior

serratus
anterior

obliquus externus

pectoralis major

vastus lateralis

pectoralis
minor*

biceps
brachii

triceps
brachii

rectus femoris

vastus intermedius*

Body Saw

Although a comparatively simple concept, the Body Saw is challenging to do well. It is good for building core strength and stability and, with practice, it also becomes a great shoulder stability exercise.

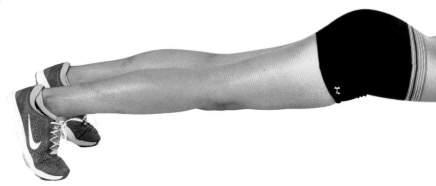

1 Begin facedown on your forearms and toes.

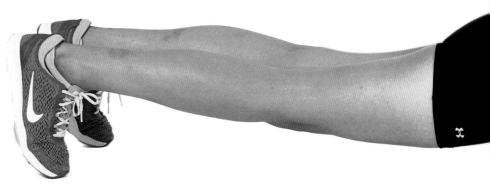

2 Rock your body forward and then backward for 3 sets of 10 repetitions (working up to 20).

Modification

Harder: Use a Swiss ball to elevate your feet and make this exercise more taxing.

Correct form

· Keep your body fully extended and in a straight line.

Avoid

· Overusing your lower back by rising higher than parallel to the ground.

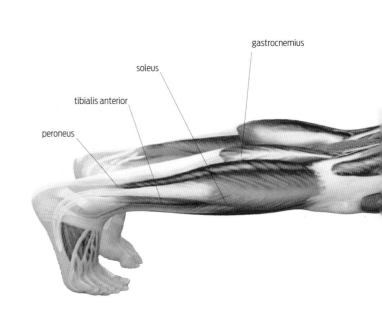

gastrocnemius

soleus

tibialis anterior

peroneus

Front View

serratus anterior

rectus abdominis

transversus abdominis*

Level
· Intermediate

Duration
· 2–3 minutes

Benefits
· Improves core strength and definition

Caution
· Lower-back pain
· Ankle issues

Annotation Key
* indicates deep muscles

teres major

rhomboideus*

deltoideus anterior

biceps brachii

flexor digitorum*

gluteus maximus

quadratus lumborum*

obliquus internus*

deltoideus posterior

deltoideus medialis

tensor fasciae latae

vastus lateralis

brachialis

triceps brachii

rectus femoris

Prone Heel-Beats

Prone Heel-Beats are an effective Pilates movement that engage the abdominals, inner thighs, and glutes to help shape and create firm buttocks. It is one of the best glute exercises you can do on the mat. The main thing you have to remember is to keep your abdominal muscles pulled in and to go for length along your back and down the back of your legs so that you protect your lower back.

Correct form
· Keep your legs elevated throughout the exercise.

Avoid
· Allowing your shoulders to lift up toward your ears.

1 Begin by lying facedown with your arms at your sides, slightly elevated and head raised back.

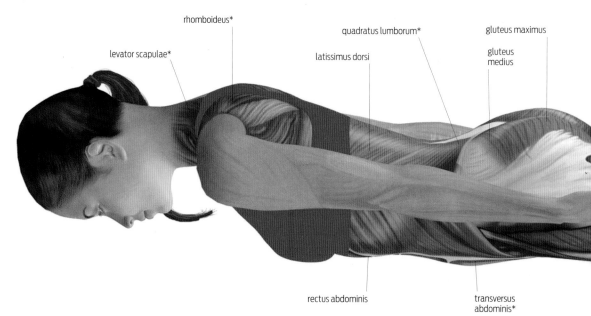

levator scapulae*

rhomboideus*

latissimus dorsi

quadratus lumborum*

gluteus maximus

gluteus medius

rectus abdominis

transversus abdominis*

2 Lift your legs and part them slightly, turning your feet slightly outward.

3 Beat your heels together 20 times.

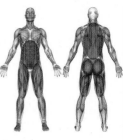

Level
· Beginner

Duration
· 2–3 minutes

Benefits
· Targets the glutes and abs

Caution

· Knee issues
· Lower-back pain

Annotation Key
* indicates deep muscles

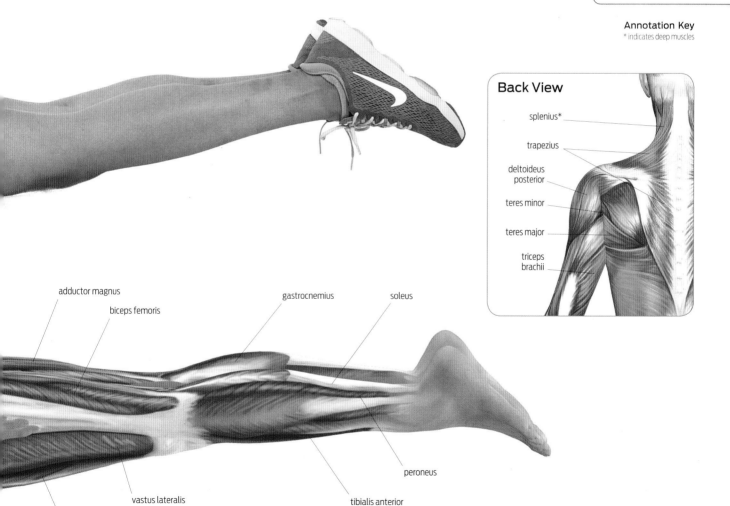

adductor magnus

biceps femoris

gastrocnemius

soleus

Back View

splenius*

trapezius

deltoideus posterior

teres minor

teres major

triceps brachii

peroneus

vastus lateralis

tibialis anterior

rectus femoris

Swimming

This mat exercise improves lower-back strength and support, along with toning the backs of the thighs and the upper body. Make sure you feel the sides of your torso working as you lift your arms.

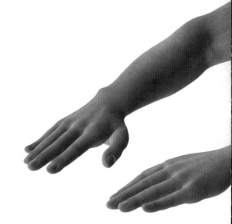

1 Lie on your stomach with your arms stretched out in front of you and your legs stretched out behind. Raise your right arm and left leg off the floor at the same time, along with your head and shoulders, then lower them all back down.

2 Repeat the exercise with your opposite limbs. Complete 10 repetitions per side.

Correct form
· Raise your arms and legs as high as possible.

Avoid
· Overstressing the neck.

Modification

Harder: This exercise can be made more difficult by raising both arms and legs at the same time. Move them as if you were making snow angels.

Level
· Beginner

Duration
· 2–3 minutes

Benefits
· Improves lower-back strength and support
· Stabilizes spine

Caution
· Knee pain
· Hamstring stiffness
· Lower-back pain

Annotation Key
*indicates deep muscles

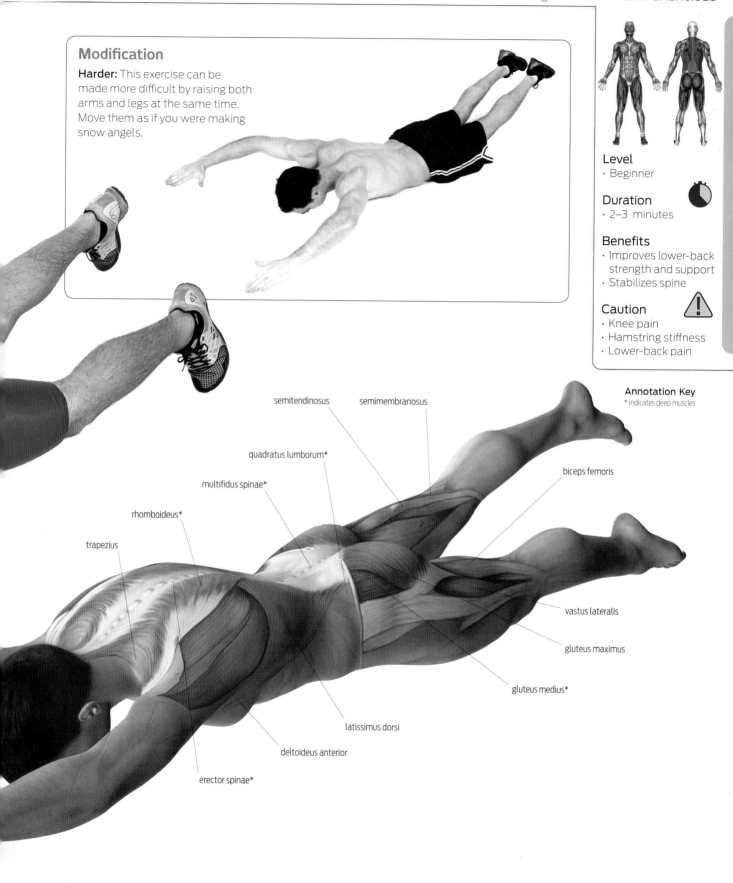

semitendinosus

semimembranosus

quadratus lumborum*

biceps femoris

multifidus spinae*

rhomboideus*

trapezius

vastus lateralis

gluteus maximus

gluteus medius*

latissimus dorsi

deltoideus anterior

erector spinae*

Bottom Push-Up Hold

With the correct use of this simple but taxing exercise, you'll get a real feeling of stability in your shoulder girdle, chest, and arms. Aim for good form above length of hold, as that will come with time and practice.

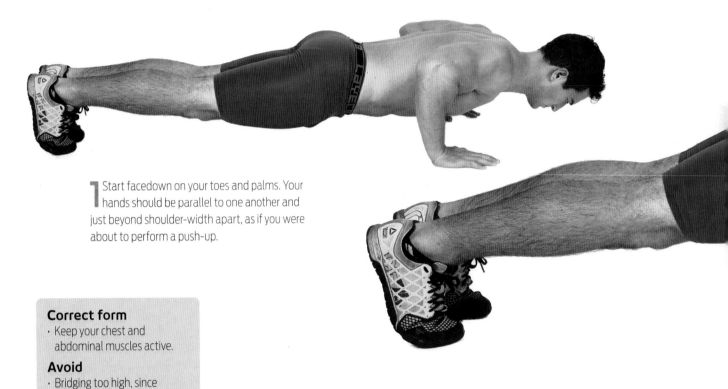

1 Start facedown on your toes and palms. Your hands should be parallel to one another and just beyond shoulder-width apart, as if you were about to perform a push-up.

Correct form
· Keep your chest and abdominal muscles active.

Avoid
· Bridging too high, since this can take stress off the working muscles.

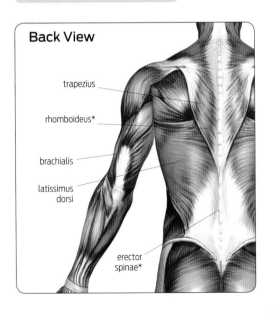

Back View

trapezius

rhomboideus*

brachialis

latissimus dorsi

erector spinae*

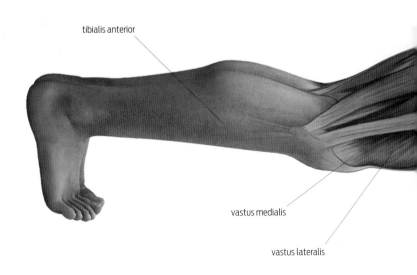

tibialis anterior

vastus medialis

vastus lateralis

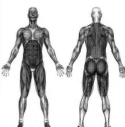

2 Begin to press up through the chest and arms, pausing about halfway to the top of a regular push-up. Remain suspended in this position for 30 seconds (building up to 120 seconds). Repeat the whole sequence 5–6 times.

Modification

Easier: The Bottom Push-Up Hold can be made easier by keeping your knees on the ground.

Level
· Advanced

Duration
· 2–3 minutes

Benefits
· Improves upper-body strength

Caution
· Shoulder issues
· Wrist issues
· Lower-back pain

Annotation Key
* indicates deep muscles

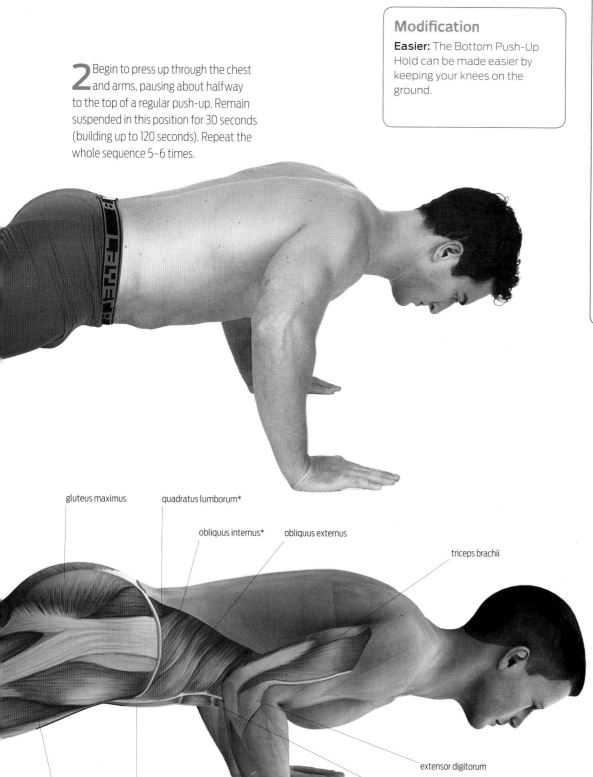

gluteus maximus

quadratus lumborum*

obliquus internus*

obliquus externus

triceps brachii

extensor digitorum

transversus abdominis*

rectus abdomiinis

vastus intermedius*

Mountain Climber

The Mountain Climber is a stability exercise that also tests and increases the endurance of the many muscles that must work together to execute the movement. This is a taxing and repetitious exercise that—quite simply—works.

1 Begin in an upper push-up position, palms and toes on the floor.

2 Bring your left knee in toward your chest. Rest the ball of this foot on the floor.

3 Jump to switch legs in the air, bringing the right foot in and taking the left foot back. Continue alternating your feet as fast as you can safely go for 30 to 60 seconds.

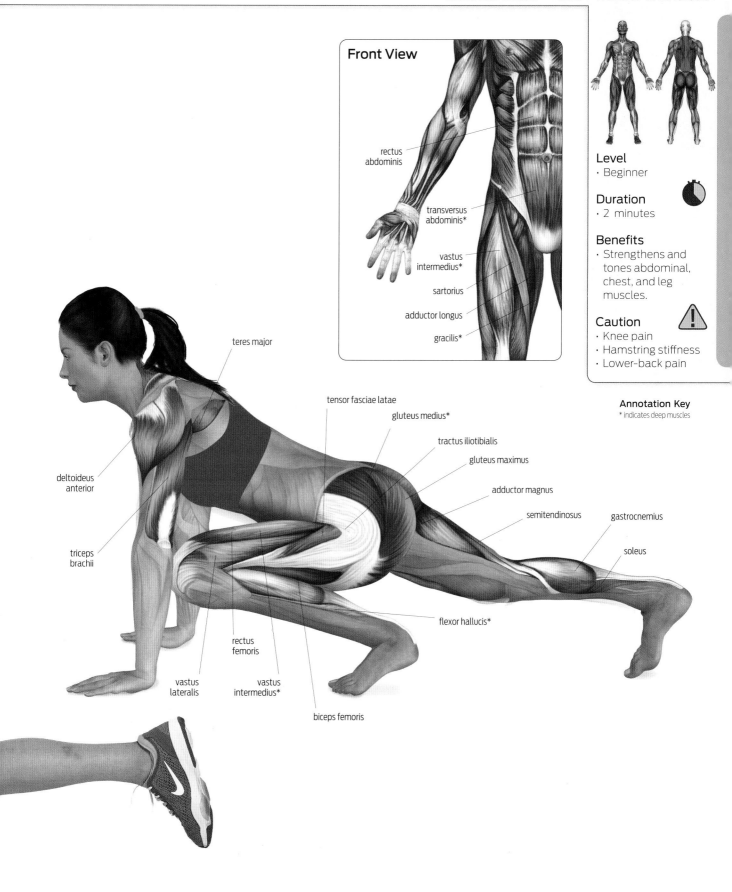

Front View

rectus abdominis

transversus abdominis*

vastus intermedius*

sartorius

adductor longus

gracilis*

Level
· Beginner

Duration
· 2 minutes

Benefits
· Strengthens and tones abdominal, chest, and leg muscles.

Caution
· Knee pain
· Hamstring stiffness
· Lower-back pain

Annotation Key
* indicates deep muscles

teres major

tensor fasciae latae

gluteus medius*

tractus iliotibialis

gluteus maximus

adductor magnus

semitendinosus

gastrocnemius

soleus

deltoideus anterior

triceps brachii

flexor hallucis*

rectus femoris

vastus lateralis

vastus intermedius*

biceps femoris

Push-Up Walkout

The Push-Up Walkout builds strength in your anterior core and lats very quickly. It trains the abdominals isometrically and is an excellent alternative to the ab-wheel rollout. Since it requires no equipment, you can do it anywhere.

1 Stand straight, arms at your sides, feet hip-width apart.

2 Bend forward and place your hands on the floor slightly wider apart than your feet. Keep your knees as straight as possible. "Walk" slowly forward on your hands, one "step" at a time.

3 Step forward until you form a push-up position, if possible. Perform a push-up, then return to standing by "walking" your hands back and pushing your hips upwards.

Correct form
· Keep your feet planted on the floor as you "walk" your hands forward and back.
· Keep your back in a neutral position while performing the push-up.

Avoid
· Arching your back or hunching forward.
· Going too far forward at first; instead, build up to the full walkout if desired.

Modification

Easier: To make the push-up less strenuous at first, bend your legs and rest your knees on the floor.

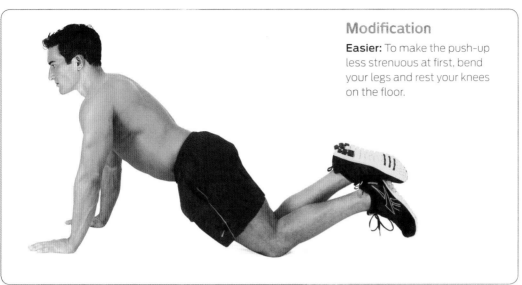

Level
· Intermediate

Duration
· 1–3 minutes

Benefits
· Strengthens and tones core, chest, and back muscles

Caution
· Lower-back pain
· Wrist pain
· Shoulder problems

Annotation Key
* indicates deep muscles

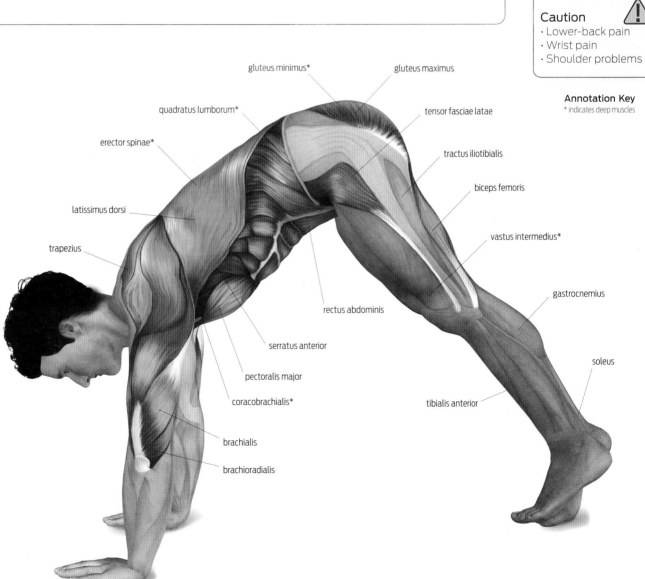

gluteus minimus*

gluteus maximus

quadratus lumborum*

tensor fasciae latae

erector spinae*

tractus iliotibialis

biceps femoris

latissimus dorsi

vastus intermedius*

trapezius

gastrocnemius

rectus abdominis

soleus

serratus anterior

pectoralis major

coracobrachialis*

tibialis anterior

brachialis

brachioradialis

Arm-Reach Plank

Adding an arm-reach to a plank forces the abs into high gear as they work to keep the torso steady. Balance is key. Place a towel under the elbows if needed.

Level
· Intermediate

Duration
· 2–6 minutes

Benefits
· Increases strength in glutes and hamstrings

Caution
· Arm or shoulder pain
· Back issues

Annotation Key
* indicates deep muscles

1 Begin face-down, resting on your forearms and knees.

2 One at a time, step your feet back into a plank position. Engage your abdominal muscles and find a neutral spine.

3 Maintaining proper plank form, slowly lift your right arm off the floor. Hold for 30 seconds. Release and return to plank position.

4 Repeat with the left arm. Aim to increase the hold to 60 seconds as you become stronger.

Correct form
· Contract your abs to have a straight spine.

Avoid
· Allowing your hips to sink or tilt upward.

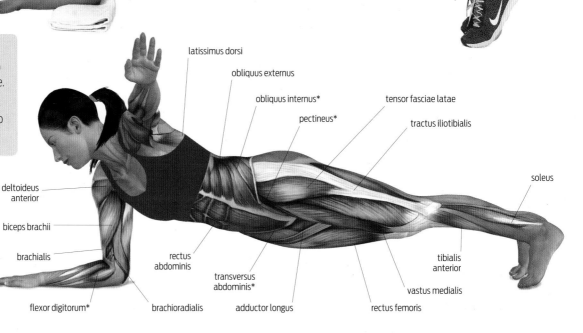

latissimus dorsi

obliquus externus

obliquus internus*

pectineus*

tensor fasciae latae

tractus iliotibialis

soleus

deltoideus anterior

biceps brachii

brachialis

rectus abdominis

transversus abdominis*

adductor longus

tibialis anterior

vastus medialis

rectus femoris

flexor digitorum*

brachioradialis

Twisting Knee Raise

This active exercise is perfect for strengthening the core, working the quads and calves, and building on the power of the abs.

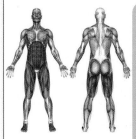

1 Stand with your feet hip-width apart and your arms at your sides. Raise both arms and bend your elbows so that each arm forms a right angle, palms facing forward.

Level
· Intermediate

Duration
· 2–3 mInius

Benefits
· Tones core muscles
· Improves balance and coordination

Caution
· Back pain
· Shoulder issues

Annotation Key
* indicates deep muscles

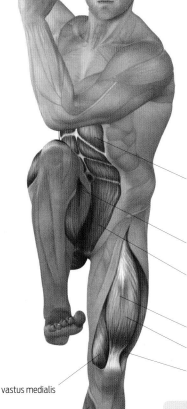

rectus abdominis

adductor longus

transversus abdominis*

vastus intermedius*

rectus femoris

vastus lateralis

vastus medialis

gastrocnemius

2 Raise your left knee toward your abdomen. At the same time, bring your right elbow toward the knee. Aim for your knee and elbow to touch.

3 Return to starting position. Repeat, alternating sides. Aim for 20 repetitions.

Correct form
· Keep your abs engaged and contracted.
· Maintain a quick pace.

Avoid
· Allowing your hips to twist excessively.

Piriformis Bridge

This move targets the muscles of the hip, including the piriformis, as well as the glutes. The piriformis muscle laterally rotates and stabilizes the hip joints, and is particularly called into action by sports that require sudden changes of direction.

1 Lie on your back, arms extended at your sides. Your knees should be bent, with feet on the floor.

2 Keeping the rest of your body still, raise your right leg to rest the ankle on your left knee.

Correct form
· Squeeze your buttocks as you lift and lower your hips and pelvis.
· Draw your navel toward your spine.

Avoid
· Tensing your neck.
· Lifting your shoulders to your ears.

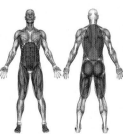

Back View

- erector spinae*
- multifidus spinae*
- quadratus lumborum*
- gluteus medius*
- gluteus minimus*
- gluteus maximus
- piriformis*
- biceps femoris
- semitendinosus
- semimembranosus

3 Press your palms into the floor and engage your abdominal muscles as you lift your hips. Your body from shoulders to knees should form a diagonal line.

4 Slowly and with control, return to the starting position. Switch legs and repeat. Aim for 5 repetitions per side.

Level
· Intermediate

Duration
· ½–1 minute

Benefits
· Strengthens and stabilizes the core

Caution
· Lower-back pain
· Shoulder issues
· Neck problems

Annotation Key
* indicates deep muscles

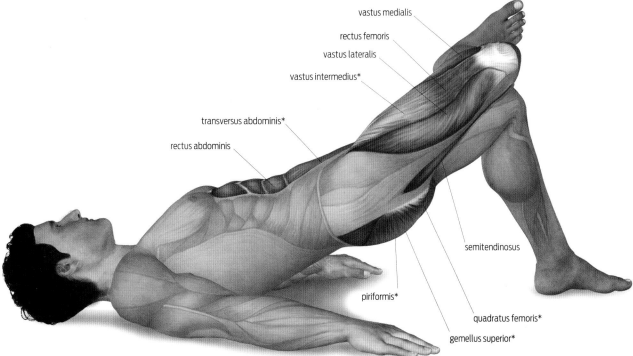

- vastus medialis
- rectus femoris
- vastus lateralis
- vastus intermedius*
- transversus abdominis*
- rectus abdominis
- semitendinosus
- piriformis*
- quadratus femoris*
- gemellus superior*

Contents

Cardio workouts are essentially about exercising the heart—improving the way your blood circulates throughout your body. Many people like to do cardio exercise because it is a way of using energy that has been stored as body fat (as opposed to energy—calories—taken in). However, cardio is not just a great way of burning body fat; it also improves heart health and speeds up your metabolism—the rate at which your body processes energy (so indirectly helping to burn off extra calories). Done regularly, cardio routines can also help to improve mental health and combat depression.

Cardio

Functional Burpee

Burpees are a full-body exercise aimed at improving strength and increasing aerobic fitness. You'll work pretty much every muscle in your body while doing them, so you'll burn more calories in less time. For aerobic intensity, burpees are best performed at a reasonably fast pace with a number of repetitions.

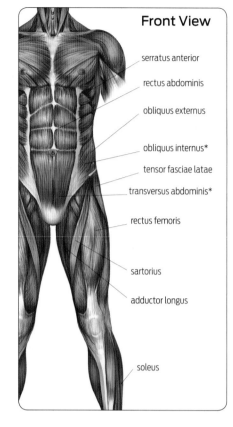

Front View

serratus anterior

rectus abdominis

obliquus externus

obliquus internus*

tensor fasciae latae

transversus abdominis*

rectus femoris

sartorius

adductor longus

soleus

Correct form
· Move through the positions at speed but maintaining perfect form.
Avoid
· Sacrificing form for speed.

1 Stand with your feet hip-width apart and your arms above your head.

2 Drop into a squat position, placing your hands on the floor.

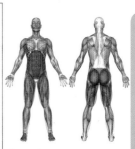

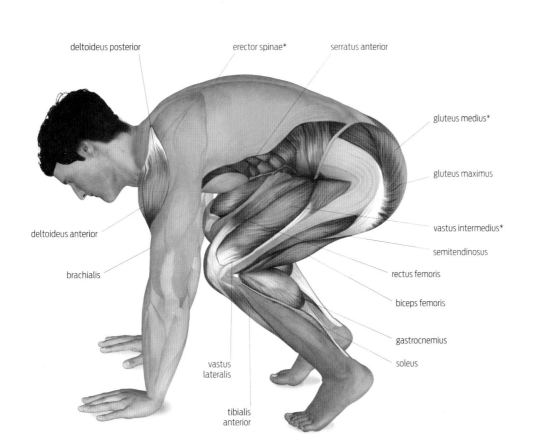

deltoideus posterior

erector spinae*

serratus anterior

gluteus medius*

gluteus maximus

vastus intermedius*

deltoideus anterior

semitendinosus

brachialis

rectus femoris

biceps femoris

gastrocnemius

vastus
lateralis

soleus

tibialis
anterior

Level
· Intermediate

Duration
· ½–1 minute

Benefits
· Strengthens and
tones abdominal,
chest, and leg
muscles

Caution
· Neck issues
· Hip or knee issues
· Lower-back pain

Annotation Key
* indicates deep muscles

3 In one quick motion,
extend your feet back to
assume a plank position.

4 In another quick motion,
return to the squat position.

5 Stand up to starting position.
Repeat, performing 15 repetitions.

Butt Kick

Butt Kicks are an effective warm-up as well a beneficial exercise for runners who are trying to improve their stride. They intensely work your hamstrings, as well as legs and core. You can perform this exercise while jogging in place or jogging over a distance.

Correct form
· Build up in speed as you go.
Avoid
· Pushing solely off your toes.

1 Begin in a standing position, and then jog in place.

2 Kick your heels up high toward your glutes.

3 Continue jogging in place, lifting your heels high, for up to a minute while increasing your speed as you go.

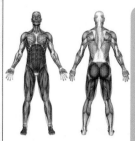

Back View

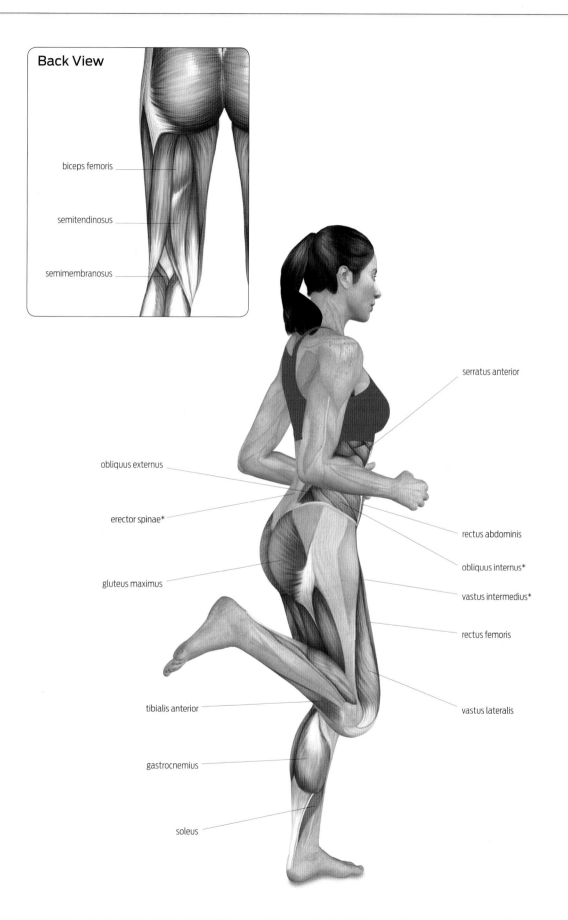

biceps femoris

semitendinosus

semimembranosus

Level
· Beginner

Duration
· 1 minute

Benefits
· Increases endurance and cardio fitness

Caution
· Leg or ankle issues
· Hip issues
· Lower-back pain

Annotation Key
* indicates deep muscles

serratus anterior

obliquus externus

erector spinae*

gluteus maximus

rectus abdominis

obliquus internus*

vastus intermedius*

rectus femoris

vastus lateralis

tibialis anterior

gastrocnemius

soleus

Inchworm

This neat movement works the arms, chest, and upper back as well as the lower back and abs. It is a great body-weight exercise that warms up your whole body and will improve your balance and stability.

1 Begin in a standing position.

2 Bend forward, touching your fingertips to the floor.

3 Start walking your hands forward with your legs straight, creating an inverted V-shape.

4 Continue walking your hands forward until you are in a push-up position, while keeping your legs straight.

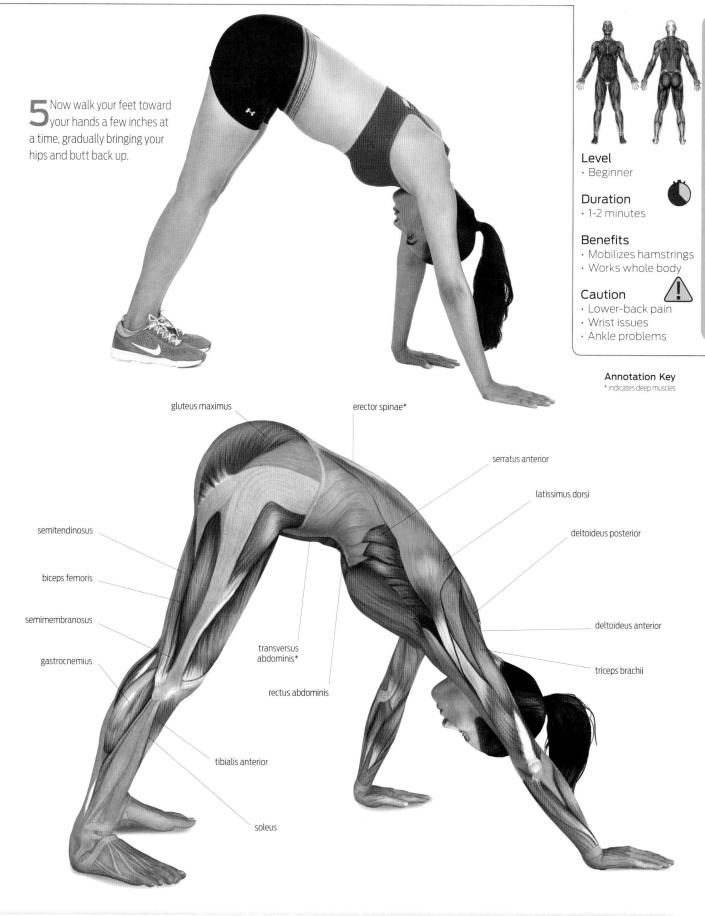

5 Now walk your feet toward your hands a few inches at a time, gradually bringing your hips and butt back up.

Level
· Beginner

Duration
· 1-2 minutes

Benefits
· Mobilizes hamstrings
· Works whole body

Caution
· Lower-back pain
· Wrist issues
· Ankle problems

Annotation Key
* indicates deep muscles

gluteus maximus

erector spinae*

serratus anterior

latissimus dorsi

semitendinosus

deltoideus posterior

biceps femoris

semimembranosus

deltoideus anterior

gastrocnemius

transversus abdominis*

rectus abdominis

triceps brachii

tibialis anterior

soleus

Diver's Push-Up

More difficult than a standard Push-Up (pages 102–103), the Diver's Push-Up is an excellent flowing exercise. It works your shoulders and chest, but is also a general "all-rounder," working everything from your toes to your neck.

Correct form
· Position your arms firmly on the floor, securely grounding your fingers.
· Aim for a smooth, continuous movement.

Avoid
· Dropping your knees to the floor.

1 Begin in the Downward-Facing Dog position (see pages 36–37).

2 With a controlled movement, move your hips toward the floor while simultaneously swooping your chest forward over your hands.

3 With your body suspended above the ground in the standard push-up position, continue moving forward.

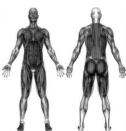

Level
· Advanced

Duration
· 2 minutes

Benefits
· Stretches chest, shoulders, thighs, and abdomen.
· Improves posture

Caution
· Hip or groin problems
· Lower-back pain

4 Look upward, arching your back and looking toward the ceiling.

5 Without stopping, reverse the movement, keeping your body under control. Return to the start. Repeat the entire sequence for up to 10 repetitions.

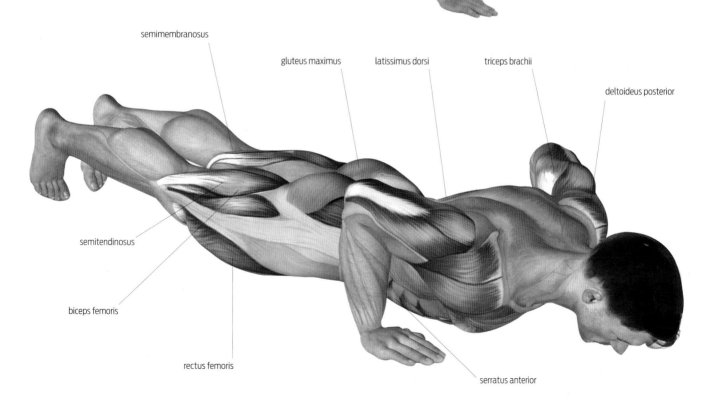

semimembranosus

gluteus maximus

latissimus dorsi

triceps brachii

deltoideus posterior

semitendinosus

biceps femoris

rectus femoris

serratus anterior

Contents

The following workouts are designed to make you the best you can be. The routines involve a hybrid approach: strengthening the muscles in your body as well as enhancing your body's overall performance (range of motion). We are talking about real-world performance—it's not just about how you look, but also how you move. These are well-rounded programs for anyone who wants more than just a trim waistline or bulging biceps: we're talking about programs that cover all the bases, and more.

Basic Muscle Toner

Designed to include the full spectrum of body movements and an overall body conditioning, this workout suits all levels. It is aimed especially at beginners and has less emphasis on major balance issues and more on the proper functioning and firing of the muscles as a whole and their working together throughout the body.

1 Thread the Needle, page 34

2 Downward-Facing Dog, page 36

3 Side Bends, page 40

4 Sit-Up, page 50

5 Bridge with Leg Lift, page 70

6 Tiny Steps, page 82

7 Quadruped, page 86

8 Forward Lunge, page 92

9 Chair Squat, page 98

10 Chair Dip, page 100

On the Floor

Consisting mainly of exercises done on the mat, this workout focuses on the abdominals and the back. Work slowly and powerfully to achieve your goal of a beautiful fit body ready to face anything daily life asks of it.

1 Prone Heel-Beats, page 126

2 Swimming, page 128

3 Mountain Climber, page 132

4 Balance Walk, page 44

5 Crunch, page 56

6 V-Up, page 64

7 Seated Russian Twist, page 96

8 Push-Up, page 102

9 Prone Trunk Raise, page 104

10 Spine Twist, page 106

Increase the Work

A step up in terms of intensity and demand, as well as conditioning and body balance, this workout showcases a plethora of angles and increasing challenges in order for you to progress and get the most from your body.

1 Upward Salute, page 42

2 Balance Walk, page 44

3 Step Down, page 48

4 Alternating Sit-Up, page 68

5 Abdominal Hip Lift, page 60

6 Bridge with Leg Lift, page 70

7 Clamshell Series, page 88

8 Reverse Lunge with Lateral Extension, page 94

9 Lateral Low Lunge, page 114

10 Body Saw, page 124

Build Your Power

The key to improving your physique while also increasing your endurance is to work as many muscles as possible throughout the body. This intermediate routine is a great way to go.

2 Push-Up Walkout, page 134

1 Bottom Push-Up Hold, page 130

5 Butt Kick, page 144

4 Alternating Crunch, page 80

3 Functional Burpee, page 142

6 Thigh Rock-Back, page 63

7 Side Bend Plank, page 78

8 Bicycle Crunch, page 108

9 Plank, page 110

10 Single-Leg Balance, page 116

Super-Fit Session

A logical continuation from the intermediate workouts, this session builds on your strengths and whittles away your weaknesses. Focus on good form with each movement and make a note to return to exercises you find more difficult.

1 Double-Leg Ab Press, page 52

2 Lemon Squeezer, page 54

5 Knee-Pull Plank, page 74

4 Leg Raises, page 72

3 Kneeling Side Kick, page 62

6 Front Plank, page 76

7 Side-Bend Plank, page 78

8 Kneeling Side Lift, page 90

9 Inverted Hamstring, page 118

10 Towel Fly, page 122

Advanced Allrounder

The key to continued improvement is to alter and increase the challenge you set yourelf. This routine is one suggestion, but please select other exercises from the book to fully engage both mind and muscles.

1 Arm-Reach Plank, page 136

2 Piriformis Bridge, page 138

4 Diver's Push-Up, page 148

3 Inchworm, page 146

5 Side-Lying Hip Abduction, page 120

6 Bottom Push-Up Hold, page 130

8 Butt Kick, page 144

7 Functional Burpee, page 142

9 Bridge with Leg Lift, page 70

10 Prone Trunk Raise, page 104

Glossary

GENERAL TERMINOLOGY
(Note: * indicates deep muscles)

abduction: Movement away from the body.

adduction: Movement toward the body.

anterior: Located in the front.

cardiovascular exercise: Any exercise that increases the heart rate, making available oxygen and nutrient-rich blood to muscles.

cardiovascular system: The circulatory system that distributes blood throughout the body; it includes the heart, lungs, arteries, veins, and capillaries.

core: Refers to the deep muscle layers that lie close to the spine and provide structural support for the entire body. The core is divisible into major core and minor core. The major-core muscles are on the trunk and include the belly area and the mid- and lower back. This area encompasses the pelvic-floor muscles (*levator ani, pubococcygeus, iliococcygeus, pubo-rectalis and coccygeus*), the abdominals (*rectus abdominis, transversus abdominis*, *obliquus externus and obliquus internus**), the spinal extensors (*multifidus spinae*, erector spinae*, splenius*, longissimus thoracis and semispinalis**) and the diaphragm. The minor core muscles include the *latissimus dorsi, gluteus maximus and trapezius* (upper, middle and lower). These minor core muscles assist the major muscles when the body engages in activities or movements that require added stability.

crunch: A common abdominal exercise that calls for curling the shoulders toward the pelvis while lying supine with your hands behind the head and your knees bent.

curl: An exercise movement, usually targeting the *biceps brachii*, that calls for a weight to be moved through an arc, in a "curling" motion.

dead lift: An exercise movement that calls for lifting a weight, such as a barbell, off the ground from a stabilized bent-over position.

dumbbell: A basic piece of equipment that consists of a short bar on which weight plates are secured. A person can use a dumbbell in one or both hands during an exercise. Most gyms offer dumbbells with the weight plates welded on and the number of kilograms indicated on the plates, but many dumbbells intended for home use come with removable plates that allow you to adjust the weight.

dynamic exercise: An exercise that includes movement through the joints and muscles.

extension: The act of straightening.

extensor muscle: A muscle serving to extend a body part away from the body.

flexion: The bending of a joint.

flexor muscle: A muscle that decreases the angle between two bones, such as bending the arm at the elbow or raising the thigh toward the stomach.

fly: An exercise movement in which the hand and arm move through an arc while the elbow is kept at a constant angle. A fly works the muscles of the upper body.

iliotibial band (ITB): A thick band of fibrous tissue that runs down the outside of the leg, beginning at the hip and extending to the outer side of the tibia, just below the knee joint. The ITB works in conjunction with several of the thigh muscles to provide stability to the outside of the knee joint.

lateral: Located on, or extending toward, the outside.

medial: Located on, or extending toward, the middle.

medicine ball: A small weighted ball that is used in weight training and toning.

neutral position (spine): A spinal position resembling an S shape, consisting of a *lordosis* (backward curvature) in the lower back, when viewed in profile.

posterior: Located behind.

press: An exercise movement that calls for moving a weight, or other resistance, away from the body.

range of motion: The distance and direction a joint can move between the flexed position and the extended position.

resistance band: Any rubber tubing or flat band device used for strength training that provides a resistive force. Also called a "fitness band," "stretching band" and "stretch tube".

rotator muscle: One of a group of muscles that assist the rotation of a joint, such as the hip or the shoulder.

scapula: The "shoulder blade," a protrusion of bone on the mid-to-upper back.

squat: An exercise that calls for moving the hips back and bending the knees and hips to lower the torso (and an accompanying weight, if desired) and then returning to the upright position. A squat primarily targets the muscles of the thighs, hips and buttocks, as well as the hamstrings.

static exercise: An isometric form of exercise, without movement of the joints, where a position is held for a specific period of time.

Swiss Ball: A flexible, inflatable PVC ball, 14–34 inches in circumference, used for weight training, physical therapy, balance training and other exercise regimens. It is also called a "balance ball," "fitness ball," "stability ball," "exercise ball," "gym ball," "physioball," "body ball," and many other names.

warm-up: Any light exercise of short duration that prepares the body for more intense activity.

weight: Refers to the plates or weight stacks, or the actual poundage listed on the bar or dumbbell.

LATIN TERMINOLOGY
The following glossary explains the Latin terminology used to describe the body's musculature. Where words are derived from the Greek, this is indicated.

Chest

coracobrachialis: Greek *korakoeidés*, "ravenlike," and *brachium*, "arm"

pectoralis (major and minor): *pectus*, "breast"

Abdomen

obliquus externus: obliquus, "*slanting*," and *externus*, "outwards"

obliquus internus: *obliquus*, "slanting," and *internus*, "within"

rectus abdominis: *rego*, "straight, upright," and *abdomen*, "belly"

serratus anterior: *serra*, "saw," and *ante*, "before"

serratus anterior: *serra*, 'saw', and *ante*, 'before'

transversus abdominis: *transversus*, "athwart, across," and *abdomen*, "belly"

Neck

scalenus: Greek *skalénós*, "unequal"

semispinalis: *semi*, "half," and spinae, "spine"

splenius: Greek *splénion*, "plaster, patch"

sternocleidomastoideus: Greek *stérnon*, "chest," Greek *kleís*, "key," and Greek *mastoeidés*, "breastlike"

Back

erector spinae: *erectus*, "straight," and *spinae*, "spine"

latissimus dorsi: *latus*, "wide," and *dorsum*, "back"

multifidus spinae: *multifid*, "to cut into divisions," and *spinae*, "spine"

quadratus lumborum: *quadratus*, "square, rectangular," and *lumbus*, "loin"

rhomboideus: Greek *rhembesthai*, "to spin"

trapezius: Greek *trapezion*, "small table"

Shoulders

deltoideus anterior: Greek *deltoeidés*, "delta-shaped" (that is, triangular), and *ante*, "before"

deltoideus medialis: Greek *deltoeidés*, "delta-shaped" (that is, triangular), and *medialis*, "middle"

deltoideus posterior: Greek *deltoeidés*, "delta-shaped" (that is, triangular), and *posterus*, "behind"

infraspinatus: *infra*, "under," and *spinae*, "spine"

levator scapulae: *levare*, "to raise," and *scapulae*, "shoulder [blades]"

subscapularis: *sub*, "below," and *scapulae*, "shoulder [blades]"

supraspinatus: *supra*, "above," and *spinae*, "spine"

teres (major and minor): *teres*, "rounded"

Upper Arm

biceps brachii: *biceps*, "two-headed," and *brachium*, "arm"

brachialis: *brachium*, "arm"

triceps brachii: *triceps*, "three-headed," and *brachium*, "arm"

Lower Arm

anconeus: Greek *anconad*, "elbow"

brachioradialis: *brachium*, "arm," and *radius*, "spoke"

extensor carpi radialis: *extendere*, "extend," Greek *karpós*, "wrist," and *radius*, "spoke"

extensor digitorum: *extendere*, "to extend," and *digitus*, "finger, toe"

flexor carpi pollicis longus: *flectere*, "to bend," Greek *karpós*, "wrist," *pollicis*, "thumb," and *longus*, "long"

flexor carpi radialis: *flectere*, "to bend," Greek *karpós*, "wrist," and *radius*, "spoke"

flexor carpi ulnaris: *flectere*, "to bend," Greek *karpós*, "wrist," and *ulnaris*, "forearm"

flexor digitorum: *flectere*, "to bend," and *digitus*, "finger, toe"

palmaris longus: *palmaris*, "palm," and *longus*, "long"

pronator teres: *pronate*, "to rotate," and *teres*, "rounded"

Hips

gemellus (inferior and superior: *geminus*, "twin"

gluteus maximus: Greek *gloutós*, "rump," and *maximus*, "largest"

gluteus medius: Greek *gloutós*, "rump," and *medialis*, "middle"

gluteus minimus: Greek *gloutós*, "rump," and *minimus*, "smallest"

iliacus: *ilium*, "groin"

iliopsoas: *ilium*, "groin," and Greek *psoa*, "groin muscle"

obturator externus: *obturare*, "to block," and *externus*, "outward"

obturator internus: *obturare*, "to block," and *internus*, "within"

pectineus: *pectin*, "comb"

piriformis: *pirum*, "pear," and *forma*, "shape"

quadratus femoris: *quadratus*, "square, rectangular," and *femur*, "thigh"

Upper Leg

adductor longus: *adducere*, "to contract," and *longus*, "long"

adductor magnus: *adducere*, "to contract," and *magnus*, "major"

biceps femoris: *biceps*, "two-headed," and *femur*, "thigh"

gracilis: *gracilis*, "slim, slender"

rectus femoris: *rego*, "straight, upright," and *femur*, "thigh"

sartorius: *sarcio*, "to patch, to repair"

semimembranosus: *semi*, "half," and *membrum*, "limb"

semitendinosus: *semi*, "half," and *tendo*, "tendon"

tensor fasciae latae: *tendere*, "to stretch," *fasciae*, "band," and *latae*, "laid down"

vastus intermedius: *vastus*, "immense, huge," and *intermedius*, "between"

vastus lateralis: *vastus*, "immense, huge," and *lateralis*, "side"

vastus medialis: *vastus*, "immense, huge," and *medialis*, "middle"

Lower Leg

adductor digiti minimi: *adducere*, "to contract," *digitus*, "finger, toe," and *minimum* "smallest"

adductor hallucis: *adducere*, "to contract," and *hallex*, "big toe"

extensor digitorum: *extendere*, "to extend," and *digitus*, "finger, toe"

extensor hallucis: *extendere*, "to extend," and *hallex*, "big toe"

flexor digitorum: *flectere*, "to bend," and *digitus*, "finger, toe"

flexor hallucis: *flectere*, "to bend," and *hallex*, "big toe"

gastrocnemius: Greek *gastroknémía*, "calf [of the leg]"

peroneus: *peronei*, "of the *fibula*"

plantaris: *planta*, "sole"

soleus: *solea*, "sandal"

tibialis anterior: *tibia*, "reed pipe," and *ante*, "before"

tibialis posterior: *tibia*, "reed pipe," and *posterus*, "behind"

trochlea tali: *trochleae*, "pulley-shaped structure," and *talus*, "lower portion of ankle joint"

About the Author

Hollis Lance Liebman

Hollis Lance Liebman has had an interest in working out since a young age. He has helped many clients on the road to physical self-improvement and has been a fitness magazine editor, national bodybuilding champion, and author. A published physique photographer, he has served as a bodybuilding and fitness competition judge. Currently living in Los Angeles, where his training methods have earned him rave reviews, Hollis has worked with some of Hollywood's elite. Visit his website, www.holliswashere.com, for fitness tips and complete training programmes.

Credits

Photography: Naila Ruechel
Models: Yesenia Linares, Alex Geissbuhler

All large illustrations by Hector Aiza/3D Labz Animation India, except the insets throughout and the full-body anatomy artworks on pages 10 and 11: by Linda Bucklin/Shutterstock.

Acknowledgments

The author and publisher also offer thanks to those closely involved in the creation of this book: Moseley Road President Sean Moore, General Manager Karen Prince, production director Adam Moore, editor Jo Weeks, and designer Tina Vaughan.